THE HEART OF DAVID JOURNAL

Leading with Vision, Passion and Wisdom

VOLUME 7

By David Mayorga

Published by

SHABAR PUBLICATIONS

www.shabarpublications.com

Most Shabar Publications products are available at special quantity discounts for bulk purchase for sales promotions, fund-raising and educational needs. For details, write Shabar Publications at mayorga1126@gmail.com.

The Heart of David Journal Volume 7 by *David Mayorga*

Published by Shabar Publications
3833 N. Taylor Rd.
Palmhurst, Texas 78573
www.shabarpublications.com
www.masterbuildertx.com

This book or parts thereof may not be reproduced in any form, stored in a retrieval system, or transmitted in any form by any means - electronic, mechanical, photocopy, recording, or otherwise - without prior written permission of the publisher, except as provided by United States of America copyright law.

Unless otherwise noted, all Scripture quotations are from the New Kings James Version of the Bible. Copyright@1979, 1980, 1982 by Thomas Nelson, Inc., publishers. Used by permission.

Copyright @ 2023 by David Mayorga
All rights reserved

ISBN: 978-1-955433-16-7

Volume 7

CONTENTS

Chapter 1: Christ is Heaven's Model! 6

Chapter 2: When the Spirit Takes Us! 9

Chapter 3: Ruined by Sin! 12

Chapter 4: How Goes the Heart? 15

Chapter 5: The Power of His Light! 18

Chapter 6: No Intercessor - Why Not? 21

Chapter 7: Spiritually Deaf! 24

Chapter 8: Learning True Humility! 27

Chapter 9: God's Costly Love! 30

Chapter 10: Come Up Here! 33

Chapter 11: Feasts, Burnt Offerings, and Noisy Songs! . . . 36

Chapter 12: Go and Prophesy! 40

Chapter 13: I Don't Want to Do It, God! 43

Chapter 14: Like Mud in the Streets! 49

Chapter 15: The Core! 53

Chapter 16: Maturing through Obedience! 57

Chapter 17: Hovering! 60

Chapter 18: The Biggest Troublemaker! 63

Chapter 19: Without God - It Willl Not Work! 66

Chapter 20: The Stability of God 70

Chapter 21: History! 74

Chapter 22: Why Are You Following Him? 78

Chapter 23: Why Am I Like This 82

Chapter 24: At His Feet! 86

Chapter 25: On the Road to Dothan! 91

Chapter 26: Kingdom Understanding! 96

Chapter 27: When God Shares His Heart With Us! . . . 100

Chapter 28: The Call of God! 104

Chapter 29: The Sweetness of His Voice! 108

Chapter 30: God Knows Us Very Well! 113

Chapter 31: Nasa! 116

Chapter 32: Is the Lord Among Us or Not? 120

Chapter 33: Fire Begets Fire! 124

Chapter 34: Holy Delays! 128

Chapter 35: Awake & Conscious in God's Presence! . . . 132

Chapter 36: With Everything In You,
              Walk in Forgiveness! 137

Chapter 37: Marked by a Promise! 140

Chapter 38: Betraying Emotions 145

Chapter 39: Finishing Well! 149

Chapter 40: Soldiers of the Cross of Christ 153

Chapter 41: It's About the Journey! 157

Chapter 42: Stony Ground, Stony Hearts! 161

Chapter 43: Visiting Heaven! 166

Chapter 44: Some Went & Some Were Sent! 170

Chapter 45: Courage! 174

Chapter 46: Perseverance - Part 1 178

Chapter 47: Perseverance - Part 2 182

Chapter 48: Are You Willing to Be Led? 189

Chapter 49: Learning to Advance in the
              Will of God - Part 1 194

Chapter 50: Learning to Advance in the
              Will of God - Part 2 199

Chapter 51: Beware of Lukewarmness! - Part 1 204

Chapter 52: Beware of Lukewarmness! - Part 2 208

1

Christ Is Heaven's Model!

"And you shall know that I am the LORD; for you have not walked in My statutes nor executed My judgments but have done according to the customs of the Gentiles which are all around you." (Ezekiel 11:12)

"Jesus said to him, "Have I been with you for so long a time, and you do not know Me yet, Philip, nor recognize clearly who I am? Anyone who has seen Me has seen the Father. How can you say, 'Show us the Father?' (John 14:9 AMP)

God's Pattern!

While pondering this morning's meditation, my heart quickly recognized how God has a pattern for His people to follow. Not following His design or the layout He has provided would be to enter a different realm of uncertainty.

As God's children, people can applaud us for our good works or accomplishment; or the Lord can commend us for obeying the path He showed us.

It is the battle of the ages to please man or God. There will be a continual calling out from our world system; it will be loud and *antichrist* in nature. Its philosophies and idea will always go against the purposes of God.

In the Scripture I found and meditated upon in Ezekiel, the Lord established judgments, statutes, and divine order for His people. From God's point of view, everything was set. All God's people needed to do was follow!

You would think these would be easy instructions to follow, but no. God's people deliberately disobeyed God and ended up in a heap of trouble and deep bondage in Babylon.

For our life to work, we must follow the pattern of God. He is the pattern. His pattern is Christ. We must go to Him for everything. We should look at His lovely face for answers to every question, uncertainty, form of adversity, and situation beyond our understanding. He will reveal it accordingly.

The Folly of Following Gentile Customs

The Scripture says that God's people exchanged God's ways for the gentile's ways and customs.

Here are some of my questions: What did the gentiles have that God couldn't provide? What was so glamorous about the gentile culture compared to God's culture? Interesting thoughts.

Here's what I believe caused God's people to falter.

God had divine order as the standard for God's people to follow. This order, if kept, would guarantee success in every area. What was there not to like?

Well, as in times past, it is the same today – God's people are still following the glamorous culture of the gentiles. They are still pursuing gentile thoughts of fleshly aggrandizement and self-sufficiency. The church of Jesus Christ today is seeking another type of gospel, not the one Christ came to lay out for us to follow.

Is it any wonder that the church today is bathed in carnality? Today's church caters and appeases the masses with a gospel that is non-sacrificial and basked in selfish living!

Let me say that Christ is the only model the Christian believer should follow. For today's churchgoer, please listen: Look for a church that still uses the bible and preaches the whole counsel of God. A church that still believes in the message of holiness, brokenness, humility, the fruit of the Spirit, and the gifts of the Spirit (speaking in tongues included) and has a vision for local and global missions.

Yes, the world and society have been changing, but Christ and His mission have not and will not! Neh'enah.

2

When the Spirit Takes Us!

"Then the Spirit took me up and brought me in a vision by the Spirit of God into Chaldea, to those in captivity. And the vision that I had seen went up from me. So, I spoke to those in captivity of all the things the LORD had shown me." (Ezekiel 11:24-25)

When we develop a spiritual life of intimacy with God, the rewards will be amazing! The Lord will share many things with those who care to take the time and meet with Him privately. He will unveil the secrets of His heart, reveal the secrets of man's intents, and disclose any situation that pertains to your own life.

God plans to develop this type of relationship with His servants and to be honest with you, not too many people have zeroed in on this great secret. Walking with God with such assurance and deep confidence that He is leading us every step of the way must be one of the most extraordinary experiences ever!

Also, I have noticed that people who walk in a higher level of tranquility and peace know God profoundly and intimately. They have made Christ their best friend, and their lifestyle speaks for itself.

Let us look further at Ezekiel's experience of this event, where the Spirit took him up and brought him into Chaldea. It was interesting to notice that the Lord brought Him to a place where the captives were. Why would God allow Him this type of access?

As God has been showing us all through Scripture – if anyone sets their heart to seek Him, they will be found by Him. They will see what God sees and know what God knows!

The unveiling of events to a human being is not by mistake; it is not by chance but by design, the design of God.

You see, when God prepares to work on someone, He always prepares for it. Things usually remain dormant until the Lord decides to move, awake, or change! You and I are called to know the mind of God.

The Captives

The captives were God's people. They had been brought there by loving judgment from the Lord. They had given themselves to idolatry, and God had to judge them for it.

In short, it was God teaching His people all the things they had done wrong and displeasing to Him. Through the Babylonians, God brought His people to a place of humility and brokenness.

Notice how Ezekiel didn't go around rebuking or casting out any devils from the Babylonians. He had already seen the intent of the Lord and was now called to come to the captives and share with them exactly how God felt about their rebellious actions.

The Intercessor

The secret power to effective intercession is the ability to see, know, and act as God would. This is one of the reasons God brings His servants to higher ground in the Spirit so that they may see what God sees and feel what He feels. Then prayer can be offered accordingly.

Ezekiel saw precisely how God felt and shared the heart of God with those in captivity. We must always be conscious of His heart and mind for lost humanity! It will always be God's desire to restore what is lost; it will always be God's desire to advance His kingdom on earth. Neh'enah.

3

Ruined by Sin!

"Repent, and turn from all your transgressions, so that iniquity will not be your ruin. Cast away from all the transgressions you have committed and get yourselves a new heart and spirit. For why should you die, O house of Israel? For I have no pleasure in the death of one who dies," says the Lord GOD. "Therefore, turn and live!" (Ezekiel 18:30-32)

In hearing the heart of the Lord this morning through this holy passage of instruction, my heart broke for the sin in the heart of believers. Too often, believers tend to hide their transgression by doing good deeds.

In trying to cover our sins, we try to help others overcome; we believe that giving extensive offerings and joining prayer groups will buy us time to overcome our secret sins!

Lifting our hands and singing the songs can't erase what God sees; only our consciousness of God can rescue us from all the mess we are about to create or have already created.

The Real Battle!

The struggle to get free from besetting, presumptuous, and overt sins is a real battle in the hearts of God's people. Not to judge anyone, but to help someone get out of such demise should be in the heart of every Christian, not criticize them and parade them as if they themselves have never committed anything unholy against God!

Now, the facts, from God's perspective, are severe and must be heeded. Trying to pacify the Lord by pretending that our hearts are pure and our hands clean when we know they are not, will only set us up for a great fall or ruin! When God is not happy with our actions, we know it.

Also, it is essential to know that God doesn't judge anyone. Still, with every principle or law violated deliberately by our own doing, we will face the consequence attached to every ordinance of God.

When God Pleads!

First, the Lord calls out for all committing transgressions to repent, to turn away from such practices. Why is the Lord pleading with the transgressor? The reason for His pleading is that the iniquity will be the ruin of those carried away by their transgressions.

How does God define ruin? He describes ruin as a stumbling block, an obstacle of sorts. In other words, God is saying to those who are led by their transgressions, "Stop practicing your sin; it will make you fall! If you fall, you will not be able to get up, and it will be your ruin!"

A New Heart and Spirit

When a man understands that he has transgressed against the Lord, he will seek a way out of this insanity. An individual can look for external ways to get out of his situation, such as changing jobs, wicked friendships, location of residence, and even leaving a present situation. Yet, all this combined will not help this person find freedom from sin.

The way out is not external; it's internal. Unless a man gets a new heart and spirit, he will not be free! A new heart and soul can only come from the One who created him – that would be God alone! Let me tell you, only a new heart and spirit will make a man understand God's intent for his life.

Turn and Live!

The secret power to living an abundant life recognizes when one is a transgressor. Understanding how God feels about our sins will help us realize that our selfish ways ruin our life! It's time to turn and live! Neh'enah.

4

How Goes the Heart?

"Who is wise and understanding among you? Let him show by good conduct that his works are done in the meekness of wisdom. But if you have bitter envy and self-seeking in your hearts, do not boast and lie against the truth. This wisdom does not descend from above but is earthly, sensual, and demonic. For where envy and self-seeking exist, confusion and every evil thing are there. But the wisdom that is from above is first pure, then peaceable, gentle, willing to yield, full of mercy and good fruits, without partiality and without hypocrisy. Now the fruit of righteousness is sown in peace by those who make peace." (James 3:13-18)

Every action taken will mirror what is in the heart. The mind will usually follow what is in the heart of man.

Let us take a closer look at this.

If our hearts are meek, then our expressions will be of that exact nature; if our spirits are impure, then that could only mean that every thought that flows from our hearts to our minds is unclean, and our actions will bear it out!

Now, it is a fact that God has given us free will to choose

our destiny. Whatever we want, we usually get, whether bad or good. God has allowed us to live any way we desire; however, there are things that we can do but will not be of great benefit to us and, eventually, will hurt those around us.

From the Heart Comes . . .

Jesus said, "Are you also still without understanding? Do you not yet understand that whatever enters the mouth goes into the stomach and is eliminated? But those things which proceed out of the mouth come from the heart, and they defile a man. For out of the heart proceed evil thoughts, murders, adulteries, fornications, thefts, false witness, blasphemies. These are the things which defile a man, but to eat with unwashed hands does not defile a man." (Matthew 15:16-20)

In our old nature (the old man,) there will always lie the potential for horrible evil. So long as we live in this body on this earth, we must keep the old man [old nature] in check daily.

If you desire to follow Jesus, it is essential to realize and memorize the words of our Lord Jesus when recruiting servants for His kingdom. It wasn't easy for people to leave everything behind, including their employment, to serve a Man with an idea. Here's what Jesus said, **"Then Jesus said to His disciples, "If anyone wishes to follow Me** [as

My disciple], **he must deny himself** [set aside selfish interests,] **and take up his cross** [expressing a willingness to endure whatever may come] **and follow Me** [believing in Me, conforming to My example in living and if need be, suffering or perhaps dying because of faith in Me]." (Matthew 16:24 -Amplified Version)

You see, we believers are called to bring our flesh under submission to God's order by yielding our lives [dying daily or killed all day long, as Paul the Apostle puts it in Romans 8:36] to the government of the Holy Spirit. It is a deliberate choice – no one is forced to do this; only as the Lord shows you, you do it!

How Good is the Fruit?

"Even so, every good tree bears good fruit, but a bad tree bears bad fruit. A good tree cannot bear bad fruit, nor can a bad tree bear good fruit." (Matthew 7:17-18)

Fruit will come out of its tree. If the tree is good, the fruit will be good; if the tree is bad, bad fruit will come forth. Remember that all our lives will be a product of this principle. With this said, let us guard our hearts continually!

Neh'enah.

5

The Power of His Light!

"Then Saul, still breathing threats and murder against the disciples of the Lord, went to the high priest and asked letters from him to the synagogues of Damascus, so that if he found any who were of the Way, whether men or women, he might bring them bound to Jerusalem. As he journeyed, he came near Damascus, and suddenly a light shone around him from heaven. Then he fell to the ground, and heard a voice saying to him, "Saul, Saul, why are you persecuting Me?" And he said, "Who are You, Lord?" Then the Lord said, "I am Jesus, whom you are persecuting. It is hard for you to kick against the goads." So, he, trembling and astonished, said, "Lord, what do You want me to do?" (Acts 9:1-6)

Here's an exciting encounter that Saul of Tarsus had with Jesus Christ, the Lord, on his way to Damascus.

Full of Wickedness!

The Scripture makes it a point to note that Saul of Tarsus (who later became the Apostle Paul) was a man full of himself, full of religion, and a hater of Christians during his days as a Pharisee.

Saul of Tarsus couldn't stand the name of Jesus and how Christ's disciples gave their lives to His cause. Their dedication and commitment to Jesus the Lord were like no other Saul of Tarsus had seen. This just rubbed him the wrong way!

One day, Saul of Tarsus finally did it! He went to the high priest and asked him for letters permitting him so that if he found any who were of the Way (disciples of Jesus,) whether men or women, he might bring them bound to Jerusalem. Think of the insanity behind these thoughts.

I think that even more insane than this is the demon-possessed high priest! The priest is there to set religious order and restore sinful man to God, but not this one high priest! He was demon-possessed!

The Brightness of His Glory!

"As he journeyed, he came near Damascus, and suddenly a light shone around him from heaven. Then he fell to the ground, and heard a voice saying to him, "Saul, Saul, why are you persecuting Me?" (Acts 9:3, 4)

Darkness always thinks it has the right to take over and moves ever so swiftly in people's lives, bringing pain and confusion to those who don't know the light of the gospel of Christ. Its principalities and powers are constantly attempting to control environments and regions. Darkness is always moving upon the earth to destroy humanity!

We all must know that darkness will flee from the light once the light shows up; night, by default, trembles and flees! So long as there is no light present, darkness and coldness will fill the atmosphere.

Saul of Tarsus, a man full of darkness, met the light of Christ in living color! This light was so powerful that it knocked him off his horse and brought him to a place of humility and full yieldedness! He didn't meet a preacher; he met Jesus, the King of Glory! The light of Christ was all Saul needed to see and experience.

Our Mission

Our mission, then, is always to be full of light. This light will be nourished in us through personal prayer and fasting. His holy Word in us will also equip us with God's knowledge and understanding. His Word is light as well. Once we are full of His presence and Word, we will be ready to defeat the darkness surrounding us and others as we reach out in Jesus' name! Neh'enah.

6

No Intercessor – Why Not?

"So, I sought a man among them who would make a wall and stand in the gap before Me on behalf of the land, that I should not destroy it; but I found no one." (Ezekiel 22:30)

Intercessors stand in the gap between God and man and plead with the Lord for His will to be done in someone or someplace [nation, workplace, family, individual, etc.]

Intercessory prayer is one of the most powerful prayer methods known to man. With it, one can meet with God and speak to Him regarding things that concern the past, present, and future of anyone's life.

Intercessory prayer is one of the most selfless acts of duty regarding others. Why would anyone pray for me? Why would anyone care to pray for someone else, especially people with bad attitudes and a wicked past? Yet, despite all the deficiencies in humanity, God still works through the intercessor's prayers.

Practicing Intercessory Prayer

In my practice of spending time in prayer on behalf of others, I find that God blesses and enriches my life as I move in faith on behalf of other people. When we take care of what concerns the heart of God - He will take care of the things that affect us.

Spending quality time in intercessory prayer will bring much fruit to our lives. It has a mystical way of returning the favor in a big way. God takes note and repays those who put others first.

One thing to note is that intercessory prayer does something in us...it breaks our selfishness. It makes us focus on someone else's needs instead of our own. It has a powerful element that can potentially build a more selfless life in us.

Let me share with you my method of intercessory prayer.

First, I will list the names of people I feel in my spirit to pray for. My list will comprise family, friends, pastors, missionaries, neighbors, enemies, local and world leaders, my president, etc.

Often, the Holy Spirit will bring a person to our minds. I venture to say that God has some business to attend with them and wants us to pray for this. What God has in mind for them might be shared with us, but not usually. Our call is to pray for them in their walk of faith and grace.

Once my list is made, I will intercede for at least five people bringing their names before God. (I usually pray for five people daily.) While praying for them, I will also be attentive to the voice of God. As I spend time in the quietness of my heart and tune my mind and spirit with God, I will pay attention to hear if any specific prophetic word, Scripture, or promise is given to them.

Finally, if there is a word that must be related to the person that I am praying for, it is now up to me to find a way to share or communicate *the word* given to that individual; keep in mind that sometimes, God will not allow us to share, only God knows why.

In closing, I encourage you to find time for intercessory prayer. There is no higher prayer than intercessory prayer! As you set your heart to intercede, remember the words of our Lord when He said, **"Greater love has no one than this, than to lay down one's life for his friends."** (John 15:13). Intercessory prayer is nothing more and nothing less than "laying one's life for his friends." Neh'enah.

7

Spiritually Deaf!

"Indeed, you are to them as a very lovely song of one who has a pleasant voice and can play well on an instrument; for they hear your words, but they do not do them. And when this comes to pass—surely it will come—then they will know that a prophet has been among them." (Ezekiel 33:31-33)

Without trying to be divisive in any way, shape, or form, one can't help but be divisive regarding our walk with God. For where there is a group of people who have no interest in spiritual matters and at the same time be another group who are consumed with following God, isn't this a huge reason for some division? I think you know the answer to that.

In the Scripture above, the Scriptures tells us that Ezekiel's words were like a lovely song being sung with a pleasant voice and done super well on an instrument, yet no one was hearing with the intent to carry out what the words were saying.

Isn't this the case in many places?

It almost seems like having a wedding: the chairs for the

ceremony are set, the altar is set, the carpet has been laid out, the bridal party is lined up and ready for the procession, and the flower girl and the ring bearer are all in anticipation to play their part, all is there, for the exception of the bride and bridegroom. What kind of wedding would that be? Exactly! There wouldn't be a wedding!

The same thing happens across America in the modern church today – everything is ready to go, except the presence of God.

Empty Worship!

I met with a good friend and church leader a few days ago. I asked him how he and his family were doing and how things had been since the last church they had attended. He told me they were doing well in business and family matters but needed to be more alert to the spiritual side. I asked him why or what was going on in his heart.

He proceeded to share nothing different than what I have heard from many believers around our region and the country. He said they were going to a church where the pastor continually mentioned to his congregation that they were one of the fastest-growing churches in America. He said the scores of people were there in body only but sadly without a heart, a heart to worship!

The worship team and musicians seemed to be on cue, the

songs were relevant, the theatrics, the lighting, and the ambiance were all there; the only thing missing was the presence of God!

A continual diet of empty (void of the presence of God) worship songs and spectacular showmanship on the pulpit will not awaken the dead! Unless these are held in check and exposed, our religious services will be lovely songs played well on excellent instruments! Our problem has been, and always will be, people in bondage to self and sin.

The Voice of God Will Awaken the Dead!

"Most assuredly, I say to you, the hour is coming, and now is, when the dead will hear the voice of the Son of God; and those who hear will live." (John 5:25)

Now, any service done under the anointing and power of the Holy Spirit has much potential to bring about revival on any level. The blessing of the Holy Spirit breaks the yoke, the Scripture reads.

I am convinced in my heart, that unless the Holy Spirit takes over the meeting, it will all be a waste of time! Without God's presence, our battle will not be won. It won't be won with excellent songs, nifty messages, and powerless ministry time. We need Him to come and do what we can't do in the flesh! Neh'enah.

8

Learning True Humility!

"Therefore, humble yourselves under the mighty hand of God, that He may exalt you in due time, casting all your care upon Him, for He cares for you. Be sober, be vigilant; because your adversary the devil walks about like a roaring lion, seeking whom he may devour." (1 Peter 5:6-8)

We find excellent instruction for the spiritual man in 1 Peter 5. As I pondered the words of the Apostle Peter, especially on these verses, my heart was quickened to evaluate myself and how often I have allowed myself to falter in pride, impatience, and trusting Him with all my needs.

Let me share with you what I got from this as I took it before the Lord in prayer:

True Humility

True humility has nothing to do with a particular emotion or a way of being. True humility is more of how one lives life and how one should always position oneself before God.

True humility means putting God first! If you can fathom the idea, we practice humility when we put God first. The opposite of true humility would be to ignore God's wishes or commands, overstep your vows unto the Lord, and put yourself first rather than God or God's Spirit.

So, let me say that in 1 Peter 5, he is making a point to those facing opposition and adversity that they should humble themselves under the mighty hand of God, which will get God's attention all the time!

God will exalt us in due time as we humble ourselves.

What is Due Time?

Due time has to do with God's appointed time for you and me. There is a time that I would prefer or rather have, yet my need or needs do not move God. God is only driven by my faith, patience, and trust in Him alone.

The challenge for any believer will always be being patient and humble. God will always keep His eyes on us as we learn to trust Him until we are eventually exalted or lifted in due time!

The Grave Mistake: Acting Out of Timing!

One of the greatest mistakes we believers tend to commit is the error that His due time is the same as ours. Too often, we get impatient and tend to act out of timing. This happens more than we care to admit.

I have learned that unless God is leading me into something, I should not allow my heart, mind, and strength to get involved. To do so, I would jump into a trap of sorts.

Always remember that humility must precede patience. Then after we practice patience over and over, the due time will come. Here is where spiritual growth begins to take root and produce a change in our character.

Be Sober, Be Vigilant!

As we make genuine humility part of our daily walk with God, know that the devil comes like a roaring lion making every attempt for us to jump off a cliff out of desperation or, like in the case of Jesus, trying to make us turn rocks into bread, simply because we are hungry.

No wonder the Apostle Peter says, **"Be sober, be vigilant..."**. We dare not cross the line until the Lord gives us the go-ahead or shows us the green light into His path or will. Neh'enah.

9

God's Costly Love!

"Beloved, let us love one another, for love is of God; everyone who loves is born of God and knows God. He who does not love does not know God, for God is love. In this, the love of God was manifested toward us, that God has sent His only begotten Son into the world, that we might live through Him. In this is love, not that we loved God, but that He loved us and sent His Son to be the propitiation for our sins. Beloved, if God so loved us, we also ought to love one another." (1 John 4:7-11)

Love is described in so many ways by different people.

Some people think that love is an emotion; others believe that love is an act; still others, believe that love is a thought and an expression of kindness.

I have heard people say that love is showing compassion to the less fortunate or extending mercy and grace to those ignorant about different matters in life. Love is, to some extent, all of the above.

I have heard in my own life that I lack love because I speak of God's correction. Insane! In other words, I should not share what God feels about our selfish ways because I will not show God's love towards the rebellious and selfish. How is that for a heavenly perspective on God's love?

Now, if we look at true love from God's perspective or, at least, at the way that love is expressed and practiced biblically by Jesus our Lord, true love takes on a whole different meaning.

Let us look at it...

In This, Is Love...

"**...God has sent His only begotten Son into the world, that we might live through Him. In this is love...**" (1 John 4:9, 10a)

As God the Father demonstrated, true love has to do with giving. If a man cannot provide, he will have no clue what God's love is about! Love is about giving.

Too often, people talk about love but will not give of themselves to touch an area of need in someone's life. Listen to the revelation in John 3:16, **"For God so loved the world, that He gave His only begotten Son, that whosoever believes in Him shall not perish but have eternal life."** The Father did this when He sent His only begotten Son, Jesus Christ.

True love was expressed in this very act of God. True love

was demonstrated in living color as God sent His only Son into the world as a ransom for lost humanity. If this isn't love, we don't know what love is!

Christ Defines True Love!

"No one has greater love [nor stronger commitment] **than to lay down his own life for his friends."** (John 15:13 -AMP)

In the words of Jesus, He taught that true love is sacrificial. Unless one is willing to lay down their life for the sake of another, one does not love God's way! One must give their life for the sake of another to enter this true love that God speaks of.

As Christ's disciples, we must understand that true love is costly. Most believers will only give until it starts costing something. Once it gets too expensive, we tend to stop giving! This is the way of the world and the way most believers love.

True love was sacrificial from heaven's point of view; true love will always be sacrificial from God's point of view, and we would do well to learn to give until it hurts! Neh'enah.

Volume 7

10

Come Up Here!

"After these things, I looked, and behold, a door standing open in heaven. And the first voice which I heard was like a trumpet speaking with me, saying, "Come up here, and I will show you things…" (Revelation 4:1a)

While reading and meditating upon this verse in the Book of Revelation, I began to sense that if one has faith to climb higher with God, one should!

In God's revealed word, we find a great revelation of who God is, who we are, and the purpose of God for humanity. It is filled with knowledge and understanding; the wisdom in God's word, if applied, will plunge anyone decades ahead!

Psalm 119 is filled with the importance of God's word. It shows us the value of it and the benefit to anyone who practices it. It is His holy word! Now if God's words are coupled with the Spirit of God, germination begins in the spirit of man. The word of God inspired by the Holy Spirit will make it multidimensional on so many levels to the reader.

That is why one should always pray for God's Holy Spirit

to illuminate our hearts when reading and meditating on God's word.

Do You Care to Listen for More?

Now, as the Spirit of God enlightens our hearts, a revelation is birthed. Please understand that this revelation is not in any way or shape equal to what is already written in God's Holy Word. If anything, the Word of God should always confirm what the Spirit of God says to any servant. If the servant of God can't prove His words, actions, or message by finding it in God's word, whether in the principle of precept, the servant of God should do away with the thought immediately! It is not of the Lord!

Remember: God will always speak through His Spirit and His written Word. The Spirit and the Word will never contradict each other. When the Spirit of the Lord speaks, it is more than just an emotion (or it should be!). When the Spirit of God speaks, He confirms what God said in His Word. Don't ever forget that as a servant of the Lord! This will keep you safe as a communicator and everyone who hears you.

Come Higher!

Is God speaking these days prophetically? I believe with all my heart that He does. The Spirit of the Lord will move someone's heart to spend time in prayer and fasting so that He may be able to speak some valuable instruction.

The instruction will be given to someone who cares to listen to what God says. Not everyone truly cares to hear God speak, believe it or not. Some people don't want the responsibility of hearing God lest they obey Him!

So, yes, God speaks through His Spirit and His Word to those who care to listen to His commands for such a time as this.

You Have to Dig for the Gold!

Interestingly, in this verse, the Lord calls out to John and says, **"Come up here, and I will show you things...."** My question is, If God needs to communicate something so important to John, why not just say it right there and then?

As I prayed this back to the Lord, His Spirit taught me that it is part of God's character that genuine seekers pay a specific price to hear. Only those who pay the price to listen get to hear! This separates hungry seekers from those who don't care to know. Interesting.

All must prove themselves faithful in spiritual positioning before the revelation can come, and the tremendous privilege to serve Him presents itself! Neh'enah.

11

Feasts, Burnt Offerings, and Noisy Songs!

"I hate, I despise your feast days,
And I do not savor your sacred assemblies.
Though you offer Me burnt offerings and your grain offerings,
I will not accept them,
Nor will I regard your fattened peace offerings.
Take away from Me the noise of your songs,
For I will not hear the melody of your stringed instruments.
But let justice run down like water,
And righteousness like a mighty stream." (Amos 5:21-24)

Amos is a prophet of the Lord and speaks some very intense words to Israel for their half-hearted worship, burnt offerings, and songs that didn't make it to God's Top 40 List!

Why would God be so turned off by any offering or song sung unto Him as worship or praise?

It Is Not Just About Giving!

Many today in our revamped form of Christianity, or at

least that's what many churches and ministers are attempting to accomplish in the name of relevancy, are doing.

Give God your worship, they say, without repentance preceding it; or give your tithes and offerings to the Lord, without heart-engagement; and the suave worship leaders are saying, it's time to raise your hands and sing the Lord this new cool song!

Much of what we see in churches today is nothing more than fleshly performances with a form of godliness but denying its power!

Alignment With God Must Be Set First!

Before one can truly enter God's presence, one must come to the altar and surrender their life in total abandonment to God. Once the believer fully surrenders in his mind and heart, the Lord's presence will visit them.

If sin needs to be dealt with, one must do it there and then! Conviction is always accompanied by the opportunity to be cleansed with the blood of Jesus! Once the blood of Jesus cleanses the man or the woman of God, they will be aligned with God and ready to experience His presence.

Unless an individual is aligned with God, offering God anything He will accept will be challenging. I don't believe that the Lord looks at our devotion to our feasts, our offerings or hears our loud singing first before He looks at our hearts and gages our intent to love Him with actual abandonment!

Alignment with God is to be in good standing with God. Not only has Jesus cleansed you with His precious blood, but there is a continual life of fully surrendered being lived out. This is the calling of God on His servants.

Too often, believers are content with coming to the church with their Bibles on hand and their offering ready to be given, and as good as this may look or seem, this is only the outer part of something we believers do as an expression of gratitude regarding God's generosity and kindness to us.

The Lord truly wants us to open our hearts and surrender them so that He may come and fill them with His fire and passion.

A Ministry of Brokenness Is Needed!

As good as our efforts to make God's presence tangible, God's presence is unique when it comes to Him manifesting His power. Songs don't bring His presence – called, anointed, broken, and surrendered vessels of God do!

In closing this word, I want to challenge you in your own life to open your heart and do things for God from the heart. It is the best way; it is the only way! Neh'enah.

12

Go and Prophesy!

> "I was no prophet,
> Nor was I a son of a prophet,
> But I was a sheep-breeder
> And a tender of sycamore fruit.
> Then the LORD took me as I followed the flock,
> And the LORD said to me,
> 'Go, prophesy to My people Israel.'" (Amos 7:14, 15)

How often have we heard about the kind of people God uses, or does someone have to be qualified uniquely to speak for the Lord? Well, the answer to the last part of the question is yes. God must train one to speak for Him.

Now the methods God looks for are not found in any institution, Bible School, or training program. The person God uses is in the secret place; yes, the secret place of learning in God's presence.

In the quietness of the hour, God will manifest His presence and release His glory to the man or woman interested in loving and serving the King of Kings.

People who speak for the Lord have willfully allowed themselves to be tempered by the Lord's hand and have grown in the grace that God has provided them.

Too often, people think that God only chooses certain people for tasks and only they can be anointed to serve or speak for God, but this is not true. The Lord does have special people for specific tasks. Still, for the most part, God desires that all who have experienced His resurrection power testify about this great work and how it can revolutionize anyone who trusts in Jesus.

God Looks at the Heart.

As for Amos, he was only a man. He wasn't an aspiring preacher, prophet, or someone who desired to serve God in any way, shape, or form. It was this kind of person that God came and spoke with. The Lord laid His burden on him, enabling him to go above and beyond his secular calling: a sheep breeder and a tender sycamore fruit.

I'm continually amazed at how the Lord raises His prophets, just like He moves in the hearts of those who spend long quiet hours in His presence. The Lord will lay His burden upon a plumber, a secretary, a vocational worker, a doctor, a lawyer, or an engineer and anoint them for a task.

This is precisely what happened to Amos.

The Lord chose him from out of the fields and filled His heart with a passionate message of judgment upon Israel.

I wonder how many believers today in our land are willing to be used by God in this way.

Qualifying Qualities of a Servant of God

- *Humility.* Humility is the condition of the heart that God approves. Unless we are willing to put God first, we can't be helpful to Him.

- *Brokenness.* The realization that a man or a woman can't be any good in their fleshly strength to God is also a substantial qualifying factor. Man must decrease -God must increase!

- *The Spirit of a faithful servant.* Unless an individual is willing to serve from the heart and to do it with the intent to please God alone - he has no business in serving God in any way, shape, or form.

Let me close my meditation by saying that as we make prayer, fasting, and studying God's word part of our daily discipline, the Lord Himself will notice it! Yes, and whenever He needs you, He will come to get you – He knows where you live! Neh'enah.

13

I Don't Want to Do It, God!

"Now the word of the LORD came to Jonah the son of Amittai, saying, "Arise, go to Nineveh, that great city, and cry out against it; for their wickedness has come up before Me." But Jonah arose to flee to Tarshish from the presence of the LORD. He went down to Joppa, and found a ship going to Tarshish; so he paid the fare, and went down into it, to go with them to Tarshish from the presence of the Lord." (Jonah 1:1-3)

How much is one willing to pay to escape the Lord's presence? Is there an amount large enough to pay someone so they might hide you and me from God's purpose? I think not!

When God calls someone, or anyone, to do His bidding, there is something very peculiar about the Lord knocking at our door. It will constantly challenge our spirit, soul, and body. Most ordinary people will pretend not to hear His voice so they don't have to act. Others will listen to it but run away from it; this was the case at hand in the life of Jonah.

God came to Jonah!

The Scripture is to say that the word of the Lord came to Jonah; it wasn't the other way around. Jonah was not looking for any revelation from the Lord that we know of. God just came looking for Him.

The Lord's word for Jonah was a direct command: **"Arise, go to Nineveh, that great city, and cry out against it; for their wickedness has come up before Me."**

Jonah didn't like the Ninevites! He hated them for their wickedness and cruelty towards other nations. He desired to express mercy and compassion to them. As far as Jonah was concerned, Nineveh could go to hell for all he cared! Yet, God has a different way of seeing His creation.

When God chooses us to do something for His glory, He is not asking you and me what we want; He already knows our hearts. He will call us, knowing our shortcomings very well. Amazing God.

Jonah Fled!

"But Jonah arose to flee to Tarshish from the presence of the LORD."

I don't think I have ever read in the Scriptures that anyone ran away from the Lord because they didn't want to obey it. Even the thought of doing anything like what Jonah did is scary. Yet, Jonah had a lot in his heart, and God knew it.

Too often, we think that God calls us because we are so qualified and holy, not to mention skilled in various areas, and God sees the good in us and wants to use us. I want to challenge you by saying that God not only calls us because we are so complete and perfect but because He knows our hearts and minds and knows that we are but dust full of selfishness!

It is in the Battle of Obedience.

In the battle of obedience, our true colors are manifested and exposed for us to see. A God-ordained task is usually a God-ordained test! Jonah found this out the hard way.

Jonah didn't know what God knew. God knew Jonah's selfish heart, which is why God chose him. You may disagree with my theology here, but I am telling you that the Lord will always look for creative ways to purify our hearts for His glory.

Jonah thought he could pay his way out of God's training methods. Jonah spent the money so he could be taken away, yes, far away from God's purpose and plan. He went deep into the boat and fell asleep; doesn't this sound like someone depressed when facing his demons and not knowing where to hide?

Why Have You Done This?

"Then the men were exceedingly afraid, and said to him, "Why have you done this?" For the men knew that he fled from the presence of the LORD, because he had told them. Then they said to him, "What shall we do to you that the sea may be calm for us?"—for the sea was growing more tempestuous. And he said to them, **"Pick me up and throw me into the sea; then the sea will become calm for you. For I know that this great tempest is because of me."** (Jonah 1:10-12)

After days of dealing with a tempestuous storm, the captain asked Jonah what was happening. Why have you done this? The ship knew the fierce storm was due to Jonah's direct disobedience toward the Lord. There was only one way to fix this; Jonah said, **"Pick me up and throw me into the sea; then the sea will become calm for you."**

When life begins to get heavy against you, when things are not coming easy anymore, when your emotions are continually drained, when life feels like you are climbing a mountain and never reaching the summit, yes, these are times when the Lord might be saying something to us!

We must introspect and ask ourselves, *Is the Lord causing this or allowing this type of adversity to come my way?*

God's Mercy at Work!

Though Jonah was carrying hatred in his heart toward the Ninevites, and though he deliberately paid money to run away from God's presence, the Lord still loved this man. He wouldn't allow him to live with such hostility towards the Ninevites!

After Jonah was thrown out of the ship, making the storm cease, God had not forsaken Jonah – God had prepared a fish to swallow him. **"Now the LORD had prepared a great fish to swallow Jonah. And Jonah was in the belly of the fish three days and three nights."** (Jonah 1:17)

The Lord could have killed Jonah by drowning him in the ocean. He could have had the sailors kill him too. Yet, a fish was prepared for him because of God's mercy.

When the Lord has an issue with us, He will deal with us accordingly. Only God knows how to do this. He is not a man who will abuse us but a loving Father who will train or discipline us on how we should go so that a peaceable fruit of holiness may come forth afterward.

The Big Fish Experience!

The fruit came out of this considerable fish experience as He repented in the belly of this fish and understood God's heart. God saw His repented heart and vomited Jonah at the shore of Nineveh, giving him another opportunity to be pleasing to the Father.

If we repent, God will always start over with us. If we listen to His voice, He will rescue us and use us mightily! He will not allow our selfish nature to steal away our destiny. Neh'enah.

14

Like Mud in the Streets!

"Do not rejoice over me, my enemy;
When I fall, I will arise;
When I sit in darkness,
The LORD will be a light to me.
I will bear the indignation of the LORD,
Because I have sinned against Him,
Until He pleads my case
And executes justice for me.
He will bring me forth to the light;
I will see His righteousness.
Then she who is my enemy will see,
And shame will cover her who said to me,
"Where is the LORD your God?"
My eyes will see her;
Now she will be trampled down
Like mud in the streets." (Micah 7:8-10)

The Voice of Despair and Hopelessness!

Have you ever felt emotionally drained just thinking and dwelling over past mistakes, which were consequential and hurtful to you and many others? Have you ever been to the place where your mind took you to thoughts of the past and there remembered your countless failures and shortcomings? Have you ever heard the devil whisper in your ear telling you that your life will never be the same because of this one failure or failure? I'm sure I am not the only one who has heard this wicked voice of despair and hopelessness!

Too often, we look at our past with shame and guilt and fall into despair and discouragement because of it. It is a battle in the mind that we war against; if we are not cautious, we will fall prey to this snare and remain in a pit for a long time!

Regarding this type of warfare, the Apostle Paul, by the Spirit of the Lord, wrote as an instruction to us, **"Finally, my brethren, be strong in the Lord and in the power of His might. Put on the whole armor of God, that you may be able to stand against the wiles of the devil. For we do not wrestle against flesh and blood, but against principalities, against powers, against the rulers of the darkness of this age, against spiritual hosts of wickedness in the heavenly places. Therefore, take up the whole armor of God, that you may be able to withstand in the evil day, and having done all, to stand."** (Ephesians 6:10-13)

Our understanding of hearing all these negative thoughts must increase. We must be watchful and discerning regarding all these voices in the air. Paul added this also to our spiritual warfare, **"For the weapons of our warfare are not carnal but mighty in God for pulling down strong-**

holds, casting down arguments and every high thing that exalts itself against the knowledge of God, bringing every thought into captivity to the obedience of Christ, and being ready to punish all disobedience when your obedience is fulfilled." (2 Corinthians 10:4-6)

We must be attentive to negative and derogative ideas that come to us daily. The thoughts we fight are nothing more than false arguments that challenge our position in God. They are designed to counter all God has promised and is doing in our lives.

Establishing a future in God will always be our greatest challenge. To move in God's plan and destiny for our lives will take faith, fasting, and prayer! *We will always have to fight for the right way to live!*

As I meditated upon these verses in Micah 7, I believe the Holy Spirit spoke to my heart and gave me a prayer to offer to Him every time the enemy attacks my mind with failures of the past, etc.

In this prayer, I am reminding the enemy that he can go ahead and say all he wants while he can do it; the day will come when God brings him to shame [she will be trampled down like mud on the streets.] He can criticize, but God can keep me from drowning! The enemy will try to challenge God's protection and cover over me, but it will not work! He will attempt to question my faith in God, but I will continue trusting! He will try to sit me in darkness, but Christ will be a light to me in every dark and weary hour! Bless His holy Name!

Take courage, all you His saints; the most fantastic hour is yet to come for you and me! Don't grow weary in doing good – the Lord comes quickly, and His reward is with Him! Neh'enah.

15

The Core!

"Now great multitudes went with Him. And He turned and said to them, "If anyone comes to Me and does not hate his father and mother, wife and children, brothers, and sisters, yes, and his own life also, he cannot be My disciple. And whoever does not bear his cross and come after Me cannot be My disciple. For which of you, intending to build a tower, does not sit down first and count the cost, whether he has enough to finish it—lest, after he has laid the foundation, and is not able to finish, all who see it begin to mock him, saying, 'This man began to build and was not able to finish." (Luke 14:25-30)

This must be one of the top statements ever given by Jesus to humanity, mainly those who desired or aspired to follow Him. Since much was happening in the days of Christ on the earth, people tagged along for the ride.

As countless followers rallied behind Christ, one can only imagine the crowd's motive for following Jesus. It could have been for several things: the miracles, the camaraderie, the food, the attention, the fellowship, or simply the curious mind.

As we are about to see, all this was about to end as Christ

turned around and voiced what was in His heart: "**If anyone comes to Me and does not hate his father and mother, wife and children, brothers, and sisters, yes, and his own life also, he cannot be My disciple. And whoever does not bear his cross and come after Me cannot be My disciple. For which of you, intending to build a tower, does not sit down first and count the cost, whether he has enough to finish it**—lest, after he has laid the foundation, and is not able to finish, all who see it begin to mock him, saying, 'This man began to build and was not able to finish."

Nothing makes a person decide so abruptly when the expectations are laid out. Once we know what is expected - a decision must be made! Our lives will be determined by what we choose.

Jesus said, *Look if you want to follow Me, it will cost you everything. I must be first in your life; if this can't be this way, you can't follow Me!*

This is all it took for people to decide to follow Christ. Some followed, and some quit! It is the same today.

The 5000 Followers

It is said and studied by Bible scholars that at least 5000 people were always following Christ. These were those who were curious and trying to figure out who this Christ was and what He was doing. They only tracked if it was convenient. This is pretty much the group we see in the local church today, the convenient group.

The 500 Followers

Then there is the 500. Bible scholars also say that 500 hundred people always followed Christ. These were the ones that knew who Christ was and what He was trying to accomplish. Yet with their understanding, they were still "up in the air" whether to follow Christ. They had seen the miracles, experienced the glory of Christ's presence, etc. Despite all this, they were undecided.

The 12 Followers

Then we come to the group of 12 disciples. These were the ones that were hand-picked by Jesus to follow Him. For the most part, they were convinced that Christ was the Messiah. They had special access to asking questions regarding the kingdom of God. They did miracles by the power of God. They were being groomed and educated to take over Christ's work. After that, He would depart back to glory. They were, for the most part, devoted but still had many questions, doubts, and fears.

3 Disciples

Then we come to the core group – the three disciples: Peter, John, and James. These guys found favor in the sight of Christ as He would reveal His pure nature of Godhead and do astounding miracles to those watching. These three saw Christ transfigure Himself before them at the mountain. These three servants spent the most grueling night Christ ever had on earth in the garden of Gethsemane as He made His final move to position Himself for the crucifixion.

Only those who are at the core pursue the heart of God. These servants seek only one thing – to please God in all He wishes and expects from them! They are passed the issue of dying to self, loving their lives more, or struggling to let go of preferences and prejudices.

Are you ready to join the core? Neh'enah.

Volume 7

16

Maturing through Obedience!

"Now it shall come to pass, if you diligently obey the voice of the LORD your God, to observe all His commandments which I command you today, that the LORD your God will set you high above all nations of the earth." (Deuteronomy 28:1)

Obedience is not a word that human beings are used to following, or at least it is not easy to do. People are usually trapped or end up in the wrong place for not walking in obedience to godly or just principles. The weakness of the human flesh is always obeying what is *fleshly*.

As we aim to learn obedience, let me break down some thoughts for you before we see some of the incredible benefits we can attain by learning obedience in our walk with God.

First, what does obedience mean, or better yet, what does it mean to obey diligently? The Bible has tremendous favor for all who diligently follow. Let's learn:

Let's take the words from our text and diligently obey. These words come from the Hebrew word *shama*, which has as its root to hear, comprehend, or give earnest heed.

Before we can abide by it, we must understand and pay close attention to what God wants or desires of us.

The Webster's Dictionary has the word *obey* to mean: to follow the commands or guidance of; to conform to or comply with.

The Lord has a rule for us to follow. He desires us to follow or comply with what He tells us to do. If we obey, the Scripture says, **"...God will set you [us] high above all nations of the earth."** This sounds like a great deal!

Now for the benefits if we obey:

One of the benefits we get is *spiritual ascendency* [dominion]. We get empowered in the inner man whenever we follow God's commands. The Lord can only give this power to our hearts. It is this incredible power that distinguishes us from the commoner. Obedient people carry within themselves this empowering virtue. It is God's will that we walk in dominion and complete assurance.

The next thing we benefit from obeying God is *spiritual authority*. This authority is placed on us once we have followed. We can't talk about a spiritual lesson lest we have lived it out and graduated from it with honors. Live out what God commands us to do; if we do it, we will have spiritual authority. Otherwise, our counsel will sound weak, empty, and powerless.

Finally, one more benefit is that we will gain *spiritual maturity*. Spiritual maturity is like a man being branded by a hot iron. Once you go through a lesson and learn it well, maturity is given. One must grow up with more than ideas, philosophies, concepts, and nifty plans. Spiritual growth is inevitable for the man who diligently obeys God! One must be charred by the fact that he has followed God. Only then will the revelation stretch one, and growth will be attained.

In closing, let me say that the opposite is true. People who only hear but do not do, end up stagnant! Not obeying the Lord brings you much pain and spiritual stagnation.

Is there any wonder why we have immature people? They may be intellectual and very astute, but they are total failures in character. It is time to rise to a new level of obedience to the Lord. Neh'enah.

17

Hovering!

"In the beginning God created the heavens and the earth. The earth was without form, and void; and darkness was on the face of the deep. And the Spirit of God was hovering over the face of the waters. Then God said, "Let there be light"; and there was light. And God saw the light, that it was good; and God divided the light from the darkness." (Genesis 1:1-4)

In deep meditation this morning, I came to this portion of Scripture in my Bible reading. What I discovered was so impacting to me that I want to share it with you...

A Formless and Void Surface!

When the Lord created the heavens and the earth, the Scripture says that the earth was without form and void. Nothing was made that we could see, for all the created matter was in total darkness.

Something struck me when I continued reading the verses as I attempted to understand God's heart. The Scripture says explicitly, **"...and darkness was on the face of the deep."** It says that darkness was on the face or the surface of the deep. It was here where my revelation of this verse made sense to me.

The world looks dark and empty when we first glance at it. It seems like it is terrible and helpless beyond anyone's ability to make it better unless it is God doing the work unless it is God doing the restoration process!

One thing to note is that God doesn't see as we do. We look at the impossible situation and tend to give up and call it a day when it seems overwhelmingly challenging to fix. This is how we look at people in difficult situations, broken marriages and relationships, failed businesses, and down-and-out people. We tend to judge the external part of the situation and ignore the original intent of why God created this.

We must remember that the glory of God is hidden in His original intent!

When the Lord Awakens the Intent!

"...and the Spirit of God was hovering over the face of the waters."

Let me show you what I have been experiencing in this portion of the study as God unfolded some beautiful things to me...

The Spirit of the Lord, God's creative Spirit, will hover

over any situation that you and I may see as impossible to change or fix and cause us to see His omnipotence at work. He will work on His design, bring clarity to us, and release our understanding of His original intent!

Before I continue, let me also explain the word **hover**. The word **hover**, in its Hebrew definition, means to grow soft; relax. You can almost picture this as the Holy Spirit is upon an impossible situation, massaging it, if you will, and bringing out the discomfort and replacing it with His original intent of wholesomeness!

As the Lord works on anything empty and void, He will eventually bring it to the right place and, in His right timing, cause it to be better till it reaches His original intent. You see, the world was not made, so it could be dark but full of light. It was not until the Lord laid His hand on it that the potential for light came forth. Nothing good can come from it unless the Lord touches something and hovers over it.

As I close these words, remember that any situation you face is not an end - it is just an opportunity to grow in His wisdom and knowledge. Once we understand that the Lord has an original intent to anything broken, we will release His glory and power over it to see it restored! Neh'enah.

18

The Biggest Troublemaker!

"Now after Jesus was born in Bethlehem of Judea in the days of Herod the king, behold, wise men from the East came to Jerusalem, saying, "Where is He who has been born King of the Jews? For we have seen His Star in the East and have come to worship Him." When Herod the king heard this, he was troubled, and all Jerusalem with him. And when he had gathered all the chief priests and scribes of the people together, he inquired of them where the Christ was to be born. So, they said to him, "In Bethlehem of Judea, for thus it is written by the prophet:

> *'But you, Bethlehem, in the land of Judah,*
> *Are not the least among the rulers of Judah.*
> *For out of you shall come a Ruler*
> *Who will shepherd My people, Israel.'"*

Then Herod, when he had secretly called the wise men, determined from them what time the star appeared. And he sent them to Bethlehem and said, "Go and search carefully for the young Child, and when you have found Him, bring back word to me, that I may come and worship Him also." (Matthew 2:1-8)

A New Order

Things were about to change for Herod and all the hordes of hell!

What caused Herod to be troubled? Perhaps the very thing that drives you and me to be worried every time the Holy Spirit needs us to make a move or obey Him in some venture or task. Let us look further into this...

One of the things I have learned as I follow the Lord is the promptings of His Spirit within. Nothing stops us from our forward movement, and nothing troubles us so much as our conscience when dealt with by God.

Until now, Herod had nothing to worry about regarding another king coming and taking over. He was fine so long as there were no threats to his kingdom and jurisdiction. Nevertheless, all this was about changing and transforming the world as anyone knew it.

We, very much like Herod, have the same tendencies. We are calm and collected so long as no one rocks our boat. If our world is not being shaken or threatened, we are fine and will continue to move forward.

God's Finger

The fantastic thing about all this is that God knows what triggers our faith and what will test it to stretch it.
We might live thinking that God doesn't know much about

us, but He does. He knows everything about everything! God knows our battles, fears, doubts, and hearts to the core! He will put His finger upon our lives and call out what needs to be exposed. He knows what makes us wake up to the reality of what He is doing.

Who is the Troublemaker?

The Troublemaker is the Holy Ghost! He is the Spirit that moves in our hearts, makes us deal with the thoughts of God, and calls for the necessary changes to accommodate His purposes.

The Spirit of God has no limitations! He will transcend every institution known to man; this includes every system, whether religious, governmental, financial, etc. Nothing hinders God's purposes from getting accomplished.

I have lived long enough to know that the Spirit of God will cause trouble to those who have cemented themselves in a false idea or philosophy. The believers who have vowed to themselves not to change will have their wishes shattered, not to mention their fleshly dreams.

In closing this meditation, remember that God knows us very well. He understands our lives and will always do His work of transforming them, bringing us into His likeness! Neh'enah.

19

Without God – It Will Not Work!

"Now the whole earth had one language and one speech. And it came to pass, as they journeyed from the east, that they found a plain in the land of Shinar, and they dwelt there. Then they said to one another, "Come, let us make bricks and bake them thoroughly." They had brick for stone, and they had asphalt for mortar. And they said, "Come, let us build ourselves a city, and a tower whose top is in the heavens; let us make a name for ourselves, lest we be scattered abroad over the face of the whole earth." But the LORD came down to see the city and the tower the sons of men had built. And the LORD said, "Indeed the people are one, and they all have one language, and this is what they begin to do; now nothing they propose to do will be withheld from them. Come, let Us go down, and there confuse their language, that they may not understand one another's speech." So, the LORD scattered them abroad from there over the face of all the earth, and they ceased building the city." (Genesis 11:1-8)

Self-preservation is a natural element in a human being. It is embedded in our nature. We are always trying to stay alive and will fight with all our might. No one wants to die! God made us this way. So, we are continually fighting to survive and to come out on top. Have you found that to be true in your own life?

Now, the life and death I want to deal with are another. It's the spiritual kind. Let me take you deeper into this understanding if I may...

Fleshly Ideas at Work

"Come let us make bricks and bake them thoroughly."

One of the things that I have always admired about people with vision is that when they see something, they are quick to create and express what they see. People with vision are quick to jump on an opportunity. This is one of their strengths.

Now, if you are a man with a secular or worldly mindset, you typically do not give account to anyone regarding what you do with your time and money. You may have a board of directors in your company but only a little more than that. Your form of government is not there to do checks and balances, not really – but to support you and your vision.

As for those with a kingdom of God mindset, the government is vital - especially the governing power of the Holy Spirit.

A man or woman with this mindset will not just build something because they have feelings, emotions, or dreams. These people weigh the revelation of God first, and through different directions from other people, they will conclude what is of the Lord and what is not. This is rare to find these days.

"Come, let us build ourselves a city and tower whose top is in the heavens...."

It is so easy to build anything but is it for His glory and with His blessing? Much of what is built today is nothing more than a fleshly desire. God won't bless anything He didn't initiate! Anything produced by the flesh will eventually reap corruption!

"...let us make a name for ourselves...".

Now in this one verse, we find the real motive for building. It was all about building "a name" for selfish reasons. Much of what people make today in the name of the Lord is a desire for self-aggrandizing and greedy glory. At the bottom of many sincere weeping is a desire to be exalted. We must be alert and always conscious of this.

Selfishness at the Core!

Why all the pre-arrangements of a preferred future? All for selfish reasons, I must say! Listen to this: **"...let us**

make a name for ourselves, lest we be scattered abroad over the face of the whole earth." This is an excellent way to walk out of the will of God.

When we begin to decide for something preferential or start to decide for the sake of self, though it may sound wise, noble, and responsible, it misses the mark that we control our future in God. We have closed ourselves to the Holy Spirit's leadership and will not flow in God as we should!

Let us walk in His wisdom and under His leadership. This way, we will find rest and peace during our days here. Neh'enah.

20

The Stability of God!

"After these things, the word of the LORD came to Abram in a vision, saying, "Do not be afraid, Abram. I am your shield, your exceedingly great reward." But Abram said, "Lord GOD, what will You give me, seeing I go childless, and the heir of my house is Eliezer of Damascus?" Then Abram said, "Look, you have given me no offspring; indeed, one born in my house is my heir!" And behold, the word of the LORD came to him, saying, "This one shall not be your heir, but one who will come from your own body shall be your heir." Then He brought him outside and said, "Look now toward heaven, and count the stars if you can number them." And He said to him, "So shall your descendants be." (Genesis 15:1-5)

Let me share with you some of the most potent verses I have discovered later in the Word of God that has given me a fresh perspective on God, His methods, and His timing.

Also, I have learned that, as initially given, God's vision will never change. It didn't change for Abram, it didn't change for David, it didn't change for Jesus, and indeed, it will not change for you and me. Whatever God told you, it would be as He said!

Love Always Overcomes Fear!

Now, let us look at what the All-Knowing God said to Abram. You see, God knew exactly what He had promised Abram. He knew exactly when this prophetic word was given and how it had not happened yet. No wonder Abram was concerned; no wonder the Lord appeared to Abram in a vision at the right time here in Genesis 15:1.

God first told Abram, **"Don't be afraid, Abram. I am your shield, your exceedingly great reward."** I think that fear had gripped Abram as time had passed him by, and there was no child yet. What about the future? What about the nation God wants? There doesn't seem to be any movement in that direction!

Let me say that waiting for the Lord to act is a challenging task. Waiting upon the Lord is one of the most incredible things to learn, and overcoming impatience is a character trait that must also be mastered.

Eliezer of Damascus in Not an Option!

In a roundabout way, Abram was trying to help God get this miracle done without Him having to deal with impossibilities - being that He was already of age. To overcome his fear or to appease it, Abram hinted to the Lord that he had an heir in his house named Eliezer. Abram threw it out there as a substitute if God would perhaps consider this. What consideration! I can almost hear God say, Thanks but no thanks!

God's Plans Are Set!

"This one shall not be your heir, but one who will come from your own body shall be your heir."

Though God had initially laid out the vision to Abram, because of essential humanness, Abram lost his way and became creative with God by suggesting Eliezer. We have all done this! Whatever God says, He will do. When will we learn?

When God moves in our midst is always by a miracle of His grace and power. He only does something with a manifestation of His power and glory. His authority over human life must be displayed first. It is God's way of receiving all the credit for Himself.

Of course, God knew about Abram's age; of course, He knew that Abram had an heir at his house named Eliezer – God knows everything! Yet He waits for the full fruition of time to carry out His wishes!

After clarifying with Abram about His intent with who would be the heir, the Lord gave Abram a picture of the future. God will always reestablish our hearts and minds by showing us a vision of the future He has designed for us. Listen to our gracious God lovingly, nourishing His servant Abram: **"Then He brought him outside and said, "Look now toward heaven, and count the stars if you can number them." And He said to him, "So shall your descendants be."**

How amazing is our God? He will always lead us to victory! If we wait upon the Lord, He will release His healing word and establish, empower, and enable us in our journey! Neh'enah.

21

History!

"Beware of false prophets, who come to you in sheep's clothing but are ravenous wolves inwardly. You will know them by their fruits. Do men gather grapes from thornbushes or figs from thistles? Even so, every good tree bears good fruit, but a wrong tree bears bad fruit. A good tree cannot bear bad fruit, nor can a wrong tree bear good fruit. Every tree that does not bear good fruit is cut down and thrown into the fire. Therefore, by their fruits, you will know them.
"Not everyone who says to Me, 'Lord, Lord,' shall enter the kingdom of heaven, but he who does the will of My Father in heaven. Many will say to Me that day, 'Lord, Lord, have we not prophesied in Your name, cast out demons in Your name, and done many wonders in Your name?' And then I will declare to them, 'I never knew you; depart from Me, you who practice lawlessness!'" (Matthew 7:15-23)

If there is one thing we must get a grip on, it is how to correctly discern false people from those who are faithful. In His teaching, Jesus said, "Beware of false prophets, who come to you in sheep's clothing, but inwardly they are ravenous wolves." The stern warning that Jesus gave His disciples was to warn them of people who come into people's lives with wrong motives and intentions.

Someone will say, how do we know if someone is for real? How can we tell if someone is trying to take advantage of us and rip us off somehow?

The way we learn this is by seeing the fruit of that tree. As you know, fruit on a tree doesn't come forth from one day to the next; fruit takes a good while before it comes forth. One can know if the fruit is good when tasting fruit from a tree. If it is good, you can bet the roots and branches are healthy, and the tree will bear it out. Now, if the sources are sick, the components will be unhealthy! This is obvious to see or to taste, for that matter. Once you taste the fruit of a bitter tree, you will not dare taste it again!

The History

Too often, we tend to believe a person with a lousy trajectory, but we didn't know it before. You see, a colossal failure doesn't destroy a man, but a life filled with colossal failures will disqualify him for the most part.

We must be able to discern this. If a man has failed, it doesn't make him a failure. A history of failure will constitute a man as a failure and untrustworthy. A man can correct his ways and bounce back, but a man who fails continually and makes no amends or significant changes to his character will continue in failure! It is all about the history being developed.

It's About Knowing Him!

Now, the Scripture says that not everyone who says, "Lord, Lord," will enter the kingdom of heaven but only he who does the will of the Father. Think about this.

So, some people come in and out of this relationship with God. One day they are in, and by the time you know it, they are out of it, and so forth. A life lived with this happening repeatedly leads to continual failure.

All I know is that a lifetime's worth of this lifestyle will disqualify this person somehow.

To add to this verse, Jesus also said, "Many will say to Me in that day, 'Lord, Lord, have we not prophesied in Your name, cast out demons in Your name, and done many wonders in Your name?" Please notice this group or this type of believer – he is convinced that the good works done in Jesus's name is what this life is about.

My friends, we can pull our resumes before God, but our good deeds or ministry will not impress the Lord. Why not? Because our life in God is not about church. It's about something else more valuable.

Jesus clarifies His position on this and says, **'I never knew**

you; depart from Me, you who practice lawlessness!'"
Wow! Did you read this? If we don't know Him, all the good deeds or ministry we do for Him don't matter.
Jesus said, **"I never knew you!"**

Listen to this: the word *"knew"* means to know experientially. This relationship with God must be experiential. We must know Him in the total sense of the word. Many people know Him because of convenience, religion, and the miracle-working power – but they never knew Him as the Lord of their souls. They never knew Him as the King of glory!

How do you know God? Do you know Him as Savior only? Do you know Him as Lord? King? How deeply do you know God?

As I close this devotion, I want you to meditate upon your trajectory with God and your history of knowing Him. Is it time to upgrade your relationship and dedication to Christ, the Lord? You be your judge . . . Neh'enah.

22

Why Are You Following Him?

"When evening had come, they brought many demon-possessed to Him. And He cast out the spirits with a word, and healed all who were sick, that it might be fulfilled which was spoken by Isaiah the prophet, saying:

"He took our infirmities.
And bore our sicknesses."

And when Jesus saw great multitudes about Him, He commanded him to depart to the other side. Then a certain scribe came and said to Him, "Teacher, I will follow You wherever You go." And Jesus said to him, "Foxes have holes and birds of the air have nests, but the Son of Man has nowhere to lay His head." Then another of His disciples said to Him, "Lord, let me first go and bury my father." But Jesus said to him, "Follow Me, and let the dead bury their dead." (Matthew 8:16-22)

Emotionally Driven

Isn't it interesting that many who witnessed the miracles of Jesus suddenly wanted to join the group of disciples? Once people saw the sick being healed and people being delivered from demonic spirits – they also wanted to jump in and be part of this excellent healing movement led by

Jesus Christ.

Most of this Christian excitement usually wears off like a honeymoon period. Once people don't have all the right feelings in place, not to mention the countless offenses that will come soon after, it has enough power to make that hungry disciple give up! This external motivation that moves many in today's Christian church to follow or serve Jesus in any capacity is usually short-lived.

The Scribe Was Wowed!

Then a certain scribe came and said to Him, **"Teacher, I will follow You wherever You go."**

First, let us look at what a Scribe was in the days of Jesus.

Scribes were referred to as "lawyers." These "lawyers" were experts in the sacred Mosaic Law that were, in theory, the sole legislation governing the Jewish people in civic and religious matters. The lawyers or scribes usually were associated with the Pharisees.

This speaks of the believer who feels that they have enough Bible knowledge and can add some value to the ministry of the Lord by following Him. Bible knowledge is not equivalency to a life of dying to self.

Many people know much of the Bible but don't know the

Christ of the Bible. They know about Him; nevertheless, they don't know Him!

Jesus discouraged the Scribe by telling him that foxes and birds have a place to rest, but the Son of Man has nowhere to lay His head.

Another Disciple Said . . .

"Lord, let me first go and bury my father."

Without trying to be offensive, let me say that following Jesus will mess up your agenda. You are no longer first; you are no longer the number one person – you must learn to take second place. Jesus must become the priority in all areas. It will be all about Jesus from now on. It will be what He wants and desires; it will be about pleasing the Father and doing the things that bring Him joy! It will be all about Jesus.

This disciple's father had just died, and they needed to bury him. It's understandable. If you have a funeral, pray that it is not when Jesus enters another city. You will miss the caravan. Jesus is not waiting for you to go and pay your respects to something lesser than He!

The Cost!

Following Jesus can't be done without His vision and calling upon your life. You will struggle to follow Him without Him inviting you to follow. People who only see, hear, or experience with their natural senses will be in for a rude awakening. Following Jesus must be appropriated by faith and walked out with perseverance and confidence. The cost to follow is expensive. It will cost you your whole life! Neh'enah.

23

Why Am I Like This?

"This is the genealogy of Isaac, Abraham's son. Abraham begot Isaac. Isaac was forty years old when he took Rebekah as wife, the daughter of Bethuel the Syrian of Padan Aram, the sister of Laban the Syrian. Now Isaac pleaded with the LORD for his wife because she was barren, and the LORD granted his plea, and Rebekah his wife conceived. But the children struggled together within her, and she said, "If all is well, why am I like this?" So, she went to inquire of the LORD.
And the LORD said to her:
"Two nations are in your womb,
Two peoples shall be separated from your body.
One person shall be stronger than the other,
And the older shall serve the younger." (Genesis 25:19-23)

I find this story fascinating in that life is filled with many ups and downs, and though things may seem fine on the outside of our lives, they are usually not on the inside. Too often, people will say, "All is well," yet deep within, a raging force is consuming the heart.

We have all been trained to be calm and collected in public, but only God knows how our hearts are so overwhelmed with uncertainty, producing most of the fear and doubt we deal with daily.

In the story of Isaac and Rebekah, we find an exciting turn of events in their lives. Rebekah is barren, and Isaac pleads with God for his wife to conceive. As you well know, God answers the prayer, and Rebekah conceives. It is here where we find great insight.

The Scripture says the children struggled together within her. One of the things I have come to understand regarding the realm of the Spirit is that though things may seem a certain way naturally, it doesn't always translate into how things are spiritual.

Listen to Rebekah's experience with God:

If all is well, why am I like this? is what she said to God while pregnant. Why the discomfort? Why am I facing these feelings? What is going on, God?

Have you ever been to a place where outwardly, everything seems good? Your emotions are favorable; you have a skip in your step; you are being praised for all your good works, and people are reaffirming you with kind, promising words; nevertheless, deep within your own heart, you know something is missing; something is not clicking; something is not where it should be? Etc.

This was precisely what was going on in Rebekah's life.

We would think Rebekah would be planning a baby shower for this great event, but she is vexed with pain and uncertainty. She would be happy and filled with joy over this miraculous pregnancy (being that she was barren some months back!). There is only one solution – to inquire of the Lord.

What does inquire mean? Inquire in Hebrew signifies to resort, to seek, to consult.

It was in her heart to get to the bottom of this negative feeling she was experiencing; it was in her to go and inquire of the Lord, for she knew that God knew all things.

And the Lord Said to Her...

God heard Rebekah's heart and told her the following:
"Two nations are in your womb,
Two peoples shall be separated from your body.
One people shall be stronger than the other,
And the older shall serve the younger."

Did you get this? Two nations are in her womb, and a set of twins are about to come out of her with opposite desires.

Most of the time, when we are experiencing internal conflict, it is usually because there is a conflict between what God desires and what we desire. The Holy Spirit wants to lead us into God's best while pulling us away from our carnal desires and struggles. This causes many discomforts and produces challenges that are almost impossible to conquer in our strength.

People who walk with God know these two desires very well. People who experience inward conflict are usually very aware of why this is happening. You and I know that if we are feeling bad, sick, confused, or hurt, it is due to an inward battle due to poor decision-making! Somewhere on the road of life, we made moves and decisions that were not by God's plan for our lives and are now experiencing the consequence of it.

The only way out of a mess is to follow the voice of the Holy Spirit as He desires to lead us out into a more abundant place.

I believe that this pain and struggle will cease once we know what God is doing and expecting us to do (we never hear of Rebekah ever struggling again with this uneasiness once she knew what was going on in her womb.)

Once we repent of our carnality, the joy of the Lord will flood our hearts and restore our countenance! Neh'enah.

24

At His Feet!

Ministering to the People

"After these things, the Lord appointed seventy others and sent them two by two before His face into every city and place where He Himself was about to go." (Luke 10:1)

"Then the seventy returned with joy, saying, "Lord, even the demons are subject to us in Your name." And He said to them, "I saw Satan fall like lightning from heaven. Behold, I give you the authority to trample on serpents and scorpions, and over all the power of the enemy, and nothing shall by any means hurt you. Nevertheless, do not rejoice in this, that the spirits are subject to you, but rather rejoice because your names are written in heaven." (Luke 10:17-20)

After that, Jesus spoke in different places, and it was evident that people had heard and seen the extraordinary wonders God was doing in the land. Blind people saw, lame people walked, lepers were cleansed, dead people were raised, and spirits and demons were cast out. All these great works had been taking place day in and day out, and for the most part, the people were amazed by it all.

In the above story, Jesus decided to multiply His efforts by imparting Himself to seventy other servants. They all went ministering in His name two by two.

When they returned, they were overjoyed because the demons were subject to them; the spirits obeyed them. Feeling powerful is a fantastic feeling; setting people free in the power of Christ is a beautiful thing, at least; that is my experience in all of this.

But how does Jesus feel about all this? What is His genuine sentiment?

Jesus says, **"Nevertheless, do not rejoice in this, that the spirits are subject to you, but rather rejoice because your names are written in heaven."**

Do you see this? Is there something better than moving in supernatural power? Is there something more admirable to God than doing miracles? Absolutely. **Jesus said, "... rejoice because your names are written in heaven."**

Please note that the word written is used here as the tearing of flesh by a lance and engraving in tablets. The sense of "carving" and "engraving" is probably the original meanings.

The tearing of the flesh by a lance is what the world did to Jesus. They pierced Him! The more they wounded Him, the more He bled! In return, Jesus paid the favor by pouring out His blood.

The relationship between man and God is what God loves and yearns for, not anything else! I have heard too many preachers make miracles, prosperity, and faith their message. Though all these are good, the Lord didn't call us to this; He called us to an intimate relationship with His Son Jesus; yes, one that increases daily.

Not Everyone!

"Not everyone who says to Me, 'Lord, Lord,' shall enter the kingdom of heaven, but he who does the will of My Father in heaven. Many will say to Me on that day, 'Lord, Lord, have we not prophesied in Your name, cast out demons in Your name, and done many wonders in Your name?' And then I will declare to them, 'I never knew you; depart from Me, you who practice lawlessness!" (Matthew 7:21-23)

When one comes to Christ, we must be full of thanksgiving for all He has done and saved us. Also, we must understand that He is not only Savior but Lord. A Lord is another word for the owner. In other words, when you and I call Jesus our Lord, we say, Jesus the Owner of my life!

Now, why is He the Owner of my life? He is the Owner because He paid the price to buy you and me with His blood. This makes Him the sole Owner! So, saying Lord to Him must be more than just words. Our hearts must have a disposition that says, "I don't own my life; He does!" God knows exactly who these are.

The Highest Calling

"Now it happened as they went that He entered a certain village, and a woman named Martha welcomed Him into her house. And she had a sister called Mary, who also sat at Jesus' feet and heard His word. But Martha was distracted with much serving, and she approached Him and said, "Lord, do You not care that my sister has left me to serve alone? Therefore, tell her to help me." And Jesus answered and said to her, "Martha, Martha, you are worried and troubled about many things. But one thing is needed, and Mary has chosen that good part, which will not be taken away from her." (Luke 10:38-42)

As we bring this to a close, I have read this story countless times, and it never fails to get me back to the place of intimacy with God.

Martha wanted to serve; Mary wanted to sit at Jesus' feet. Martha was distracted with much serving; Mary was mesmerized by the words of Jesus. Martha was corrected; Mary was praised and favored by Christ.

In other words, we don't get to know God's mind and heart by just coming to church, by only reading our Bible, or by getting prayed for. The mind and spirit of God come through spending lengthy time in prayer and solitude before God.

We wait for His will to be delivered to us at this place. This is where all our issues in life and our decision (personal and business) will be weighed out. Nothing substitutes prayer like sitting and waiting at His feet. Neh'enah.

25

On the Road to Dothan!

"Then his brothers went to feed their father's flock in Shechem. And Israel told Joseph, "Are not your brothers feeding the flock in Shechem? Come, I will send you to them." So, he said to him, "Here I am." Then he said to him, "Please go and see if it is well with your brothers and well with the flocks and bring back word to me." So, he sent him out of the Valley of Hebron, and he went to Shechem. Now a confident man found him, and there he was, wandering in the field. And the man asked him, saying, "What are you seeking?" So, he said, "I am seeking my brothers. Please tell me where they are feeding their flocks." And the man said, "They have departed from here, for I heard them say, 'Let us go to Dothan.'" So, Joseph went after his brothers and found them in Dothan." (Genesis 37:12-17)

As I have been learning intentionally to walk with God on a day-to-day basis, I have come to know that the Lord will always lead us to places of personal development affecting us on so many levels: spiritually, emotionally, economically, socially, and other areas that produce character in us.

In the areas I just mentioned, we are either learning to improve at them or somehow stuck in a world of bitterness and feeling incomplete because we can't overcome the obstacle or graduate from the hard-learned lessons.

We Must Trust God

In living this life out with God, we must live it out by faith. It must be a faith that brings confidence to our inner man, a belief that assures us that our lives will be cared for by a loving heavenly Father.

As we learn to trust Him, we will also allow ourselves to be led by Him. You see, God has our best interest at heart always! He doesn't allow anything to come and hurt us, destroy us, or overtake us. Everything we go through in our lives is hand-picked and hand-crafted by God. Never doubt the Lord's workings!

With this said, let me show you a fantastic man named Joseph; he was the first son of Jacob, the patriarch. His calling, journey with God, and promotion are depicted beautifully in the Scriptures.

It came to pass that Jacob had his first son with Rachel, and they named him Joseph. Jacob and Rachel loved this young man and probably more than all the other children they had for various reasons.

The Scripture says that Jacob favored Joseph and gave him

a coat of many colors. This colorful coat distinguished this young man from his siblings; is it any wonder why his brother's envy and jealousy were manifest?

The siblings somehow decided to get rid of this young man but didn't know how.

In Joseph's World

Joseph was oblivious to his brothers' sentiments and didn't see anything wrong with anything. He was a happy-go-lucky seventeen-year-old who felt blessed and enriched by his father's favor.

One day this was all about to change. Yet, Joseph was clueless about anything negative around him.

This seems to be the posture of many believers today – clueless about the dealings of God's hand.

Entering the Furnace

The Scripture continues to say that one day Joseph went looking for his brothers, and his father told him they were caring for sheep in Shechem. So, Jacob sent Joseph to Shechem so that he would be with them.

When he got to Shechem, he noticed they were not there, but a man told him they had moved to Dothan to take care of the sheep over at that town about 12 to 15 miles north of Shechem.

Why is Dothan so important? It is essential because this was the last town he would be at with his brothers before his brothers put him away and finally sold him as a slave to some Ishmaelites heading to Egypt, where he would later be sold as a slave.

What happened to the Dream?

In heading to Dothan, Jacob and Joseph's good intention was to be with his brothers and perhaps help them somehow with the sheep. Yet, at the same time, God had other plans.

It is the plans of God that change the course of destiny in any setting. Humanity always plans the future the best way he knows; however, God always has the last word in everything. Any man who walks with God must come to this understanding.

The Scripture says, **"A man's mind plans his way** [as he journeys through life], **But the LORD directs his steps and establishes them."** (Proverbs 16:9 AMP)

In this message, I want you to see how the Lord will bring all our dreams to a place called Dothan. It's the place of altering, the site of death, the position of surrender and humility; it is the place of more profound brokenness.

The next move of God in your life might be to Dothan. When you discover it, know that God is up to something great for your life! Neh'enah.

26

Kingdom Understanding!

"Therefore, hear the parable of the sower: When anyone hears the word of the kingdom and does not understand it, then the wicked one comes and snatches away what was sown in his heart." (Matthew 13:18, 19)

While praying and meditating upon this portion of Scripture, the Holy Spirit once again came to me to teach me the story of the sower and what he purposed to do upon the fields.

Jesus spoke in parables to those who followed him, and here again, there is no exception as He unfolded a heavenly truth using a natural everyday story.

In this portion of Scripture, Jesus tells the story of the sower who threw seeds by the wayside: **"Behold, a sower went out to sow. And as he sowed, some seed fell by the wayside; and the birds came and devoured them."** (v. 3, 4)

It would be to our advantage to listen to the words of Jesus as He unfolds this truth, and why was it that the first attempt to plant didn't produce anything?

What does it mean to throw seeds by the wayside? What was He teaching us? What was the idea behind this first failed attempt to plant seed?

Listen to what Christ defines this one seed falling by the wayside: Jesus likened it to **"...anyone who hears the word of the kingdom, and does not understand it, the wicked one comes and snatches away what was sown in his heart."**

Understanding the Word of the Kingdom

In short, this seed fell by the wayside and was never sowed in the ground. In other words, the word the Spirit of God gave was never adopted, engrafted, and embedded into the heart of the hearer. It seems like this one seed never made it underground; therefore, a bird saw the seed, took it, and ate it!

Jesus was teaching us that if the word of the kingdom is not understood, it will profit nothing!

Now, let us see the meaning of this word, understand. The word know in this context means primarily "to bring together," "to come together," or "to come to an agreement," and "to accept something by hearing."

The Lord was speaking to the spirit of man and, in essence, was telling him, "If you don't bring together or come together or come to an agreement in all that I am saying to you, you will not receive the benefit of what I am trying to do in you. You must not only agree, but you also must accept what I'm telling you!" Do you see this?

Too often, we try to understand God with our human logic; we make a feeble attempt to understand from an earthly perspective what the Lord is saying. Remember: God does not think like us!

When I speak of understanding what the Lord is saying, I'm referring to understanding God's plan as He has designed it for you. This is not a general plan but a personally tailored one He has made specifically for you!

This includes His will, emotions, heart, passion, and the power to persevere and see it come to fruition in His time.

If We Understand What He is Saying...

If we understand what God is specifically saying to us, we will reap a great harvest. Always remember that the Lord is more interested in us learning the lesson than getting what we ask.

Now, I know some people would probably disagree with my theology on this, but allow God to teach you, His ways. His first and foremost desire is to transform us into the image of His Son, Jesus. His goal is to develop the person of

Christ in us; to this end, the Spirit of God will always lead us. Neh'enah.

27

When God Shares His Heart with Us!

"Now Jesus called His disciples to Himself and said, "I have compassion on the multitude, because they have now continued with Me three days and have nothing to eat. And I do not want to send them away hungry, lest they faint on the way." Then His disciples asked Him, "Where could we get enough bread in the wilderness to fill such a great multitude?" Jesus said to them, "How many loaves do you have?" And they said, "Seven, and a few little fish." (Matthew 15:32-34)

While praying and meditating this morning, I came across this specific story.

You might have read how Jesus fed the multitudes with just a few loaves and fish. It is one of the most powerful and miraculous signs Jesus did during His earthly ministry.

As I continued in His word, I felt the Holy Spirit opening my eyes to see something I had never seen before; I saw the heart of God in need. In need of what you might ask, well, in need of feeding hungry people, in need of catching someone to pick up the burden and do something about it. I'm sure you understand what I am talking about. Too often, this seems to be the case with many believers today. We hear the burden of the Lord and see the need, but that is as far as that passion goes. After we know where the Lord is fixing our eyes on, we conclude that we can't help in that area. The excuses vary: the demand is too much for us to carry out, too expensive, not convenient for our life or lifestyle, etc.

God Always Carries a Burden

When we tune in with the Lord, He will disclose His heart and mind to us. He will let us see what is bothering, hurting, or concerning Him. He tends to share this with people who care to listen. You will know that this is the minority. Most people are too busy trying to get their needs met to sit in God's presence. Spending a good hour in the quiet time of worship and prayer is almost impossible for some. People don't care what is happening in Christ's heart so long as their needs are met.

The idea that people are enrolled with membership at a local church is meaningless to God if you can't hear His burden. Attending church and doing your duty is only part of what God expects from us; He is looking for people who will see, hear, and think as He does. It is here where the most significant impact is made!

It's Too Big for Us!

Without anyone asking this one disciple, he jumped and said, **"Where could we get enough bread in the wilderness to fill such a great multitude?"** What a great question. What a great observation! He was probably one of the disciples who understood numbers, etc.

He heard the heart of God and felt His need; he saw the mass of people and the location where they were standing. His intellectual mind did the math and concluded, "Where can we get enough bread…?"

Please understand that you and I are continually invited to make these same assessments in our lives.

Too many don't tune in to the Lord's heart because they know that if they did, their lives would never be the same! If we tune in to the Holy Spirit, He will reveal what God expects from us. Once we hear God, we become responsible for doing His will.

It Is God Who Sponsors!

If God shows us something out of the ordinary that challenges our lifestyle, know that God has every intention to walk with you and get you through this experience. He will not leave us to fight alone but will always accompany us with His Spirit.

It is nothing for God to give us the resources or use what

we have to keep touching lives for His glory. Will you offer God all you have so that He may multiply it for His glory? Neh'enah.

28

The Call of God!

"Now, therefore, behold, the cry of the children of Israel has come to Me, and I have also seen the oppression with which the Egyptians oppress them. Come now, therefore, and I will send you to Pharaoh that you may bring My people, the children of Israel, out of Egypt." But Moses said to God, "Who am I that I should go to Pharaoh and that I should bring the children of Israel out of Egypt?" So, He said, "I will certainly be with you." (Exodus 3:9-12)

In the call of God, one must realize that it is God's call upon a human vessel, not the ship having a bright idea of how to serve God. Too many people are trying to serve God without God first prompting them to do so.

There are a few things that I have picked up in my spirit as I read these few verses regarding serving God. Let me share them with you.

First, we must realize that God has called us to have a personal and intimate relationship with Him. This is the call for every believer. This is the highest call and most needed of all forms of worship.

Once a servant of the Lord begins to walk with God at this level, whether knowingly or unknowingly, he is positioning himself for a visitation from the Lord. For some reason, God looks at a man's work ethic as a preliminary before He meets with him, either by a dream, revelation, trance, or direct encounter.

In the case of this specific calling, Moses had lived in Egypt for 40 years, where he learned the ways of the Egyptians. He served in their local government but knew deep within that he was called for something greater. Moses took it upon himself to kill an Egyptian who was fighting with one of his Hebrew brothers, and the matter was found out by Pharaoh, who wanted to kill him for it. It was due to this that Moses fled to Midian.

After spending 40 years in Midian, now married, and tending his father-in-law's sheep, he came to Horeb the mountain of God, where he saw the burning bush. God spoke to him out of this bush and commissioned him to go and deliver His people, the children of Israel.

The Call

When God calls us, He does it with people he can trust. The people God calls understand the nature of the calling and are called to go and take care of God's wishes. Yes, the spirit is willing, but the flesh is weak! The challenges are many.

As imperfect, incomplete, and unworthy Moses might have felt, God was willing to take a chance on this one servant.

God will always share His secrets, wishes, and most profound burdens with those who care to listen!

Jehovah God said to Moses, **"...the cry of the children of Israel has come to Me, and I have also seen the oppression with which the Egyptians oppress them. Come now, therefore, and I will send you to Pharaoh..."** After laying out His one desire for His people before Moses, God challenged Moses as the vessel.

Who Am I That I Should Go?

What a great question Moses asked the Lord. I would have asked the same: **"Who am I that I should go to Pharaoh and that I should bring the children of Israel out of Egypt?"** Can you imagine God laying out before Moses and telling him, "I want you to go and deliver them?" Mind you, Moses was wanted in Egypt for killing a man! God wasn't making any sense. But does He ever?

God needed a man whom the crises of life had emptied; He needed a man who was no longer dependent upon his wisdom and knowledge; He was looking for a man who was humble enough to hear and obey God – yes, Moses was this man!

So, **He said, "I will certainly be with you."**

The Lord told Moses to go and deliver His people from Egyptian bondage. It was understood that all other resources would be coming in as Moses needed. But to prove a point of fleshly elements at work, Moses quickly felt responsible for getting the job done in his power!

It wasn't our idea, so we are not responsible for the resources. It was God's idea, so He was responsible for bringing in the resources to produce a harvest. When we take responsibility away from God for His calling, we will fail miserably.

When God calls us, He provides purpose, vision, and provision. God is the resource for all He commands us to do.

Such resulted from the calling of Moses and His ministry as the deliverer of Israel from Egyptian bondage; so, it will be with us in like manner. Neh'enah.

29

The Sweetness of His Voice!

"Now it was the Feast of Dedication in Jerusalem, and it was winter. And Jesus walked into the temple on Solomon's porch. Then the Jews surrounded Him and said to Him, "How long do You keep us in doubt? If You are the Christ, tell us." Jesus answered them, "I told you, and you do not believe. The works that I do in My Father's name, they bear witness of Me. But you do not believe because you are not of My sheep, as I said to you. My sheep hear My voice; I know them, and they follow Me. And I give them eternal life, and they shall never perish; neither shall anyone snatch them out of My hand. My Father, who has given them to Me, is greater than all; and no one can snatch them out of My Father's hand. My Father and I are one." (John 10:22-30)

"There are, it may be, so many kinds of voices in the world, and no kind is without signification." (1 Corinthians 14:10)

As I begin unfolding this meditation that the Lord has brought to my mind and heart, please allow the Spirit of God to bring you closer to His plan and purpose.

In John 10, the Lord says something about His sheep. This

is not regarding those sheep who are not His, but His sheep. His sheep are characterized by one thing: they hear His voice!

Jesus continues to say that the Shepherd knows His sheep, and His sheep follow Him. An intimate relationship with God and His Spirit is a sure guarantee to live and walk in the life of God.

Now, too often, we don't want to hear His voice, or we don't want to listen to His voice. Other times, we can't hear His voice due to other things that hold our attention.

Let me say this: His voice sure guarantees to lead us through anything and everything in life. He will lead us through difficulty, testing, hardships, and adversity.

As we only try to hear God's voice, we must recognize and quickly process other agents.

Beware of Other Voices!

The Scripture says, **"There may be, so many kinds of voices in the world, and no kind is without signification."** What does this mean?

Agents that have different motives, other intentions, another purpose. This means that there are other voices also fighting for your attention. If the voice comes from a source other than the Holy Spirit or God's word, it probably is not good. It plans to draw you away from God and lead you astray to a world you can't handle.

We must learn to practice spiritual discernment. What is discernment? Discernment is the ability to recognize small details, accurately tell the difference between similar things, and make intelligent judgments using such observations—a keen perception of review.

In walking with God and being led by His Spirit, who talks to us, we must perceive what the Spirit of God might be saying to us. Is what we hear bringing us closer to Jesus or drawing us away from Jesus?

His Word Carries Us!

"Immediately Jesus made the disciples get into the boat and go ahead of him to the other side, while he dismissed the crowd. After he had dismissed them, he went up on a mountainside by himself to pray. Later that night, he was there alone, and the boat was already a considerable distance from land, buffeted by the waves because the wind was against it. Shortly before dawn Jesus went out to them, walking on the lake. When the disciples saw him walking on the lake, they were terrified. "It's a ghost," they said, and cried out in fear. But Jesus immediately said to them: "Take courage! It is I. Don't be afraid." "Lord, if it's you," Peter replied, "tell me to come

to you on the water." "Come," he said. Then Peter got down out of the boat, walked on the water and came toward Jesus. But when he saw the wind, he was afraid and, beginning to sink, cried out, "Lord, save me!" (Matthew 14:22-30)

In our story above, we learn that Christ came to the disciples late at night while they were on the boat. They didn't recognize Him. As Jesus walked on water, they thought He was a ghost and became afraid of this person to the point that they cried out for fear. Jesus said to the disciples, **"Take courage! It is I. Don't be afraid."**

At this moment, **Peter said, "Lord, if it's you, tell me to come to you on the water." Jesus said, "Come."**

Peter began to walk on water but then lost God's word somewhere; he started looking at the wind instead of His word....and began to sink!

This and more will happen to anyone who doesn't follow or stick to His word. No one has the answer to everything – only Jesus! We need to hear His word; we need to focus on His word; we need to obey His word and trust that He will bring us through!

The Secret to Perfect Peace!

"You will keep in [a] perfect and constant peace the one

whose mind is steadfast [that is, committed and focused on You—in both [b]inclination and character], **because he trusts and takes refuge in You** [with hope and confident expectation]." (Isaiah 26:3)

As I close this meditation today, I want you to know and understand that when one hears His voice and allows God's voice to permeate our mind and heart, an overwhelming sense of peace will come upon us.

Once we know that we have heard God, we also know that God has heard you and seen your commitment to stand firm.

His voice will always take us through anything and everything! Neh'enah.

30

God Knows Us Very Well!

"Then it came to pass when Pharaoh had let the people go, that God did not lead them by way of the land of the Philistines, although that was near; for God said, "Lest perhaps the people change their minds when they see war and return to Egypt." So, God led the people around by way of the wilderness of the Red Sea." (Exodus 13:17, 18)

The title of my devotion today is an understatement, I know. Yet, we must realize that this statement is more accurate than real can be. God knows us very well, indeed. He knows our inner parts. He knows our aspirations, desires, and dreams but Also our fears, doubts, and weaknesses. This is the God we serve.

Despite God's knowledge of us, He still commands and sends us out to represent Him. He equips us with Himself and fills our lives with His glory and supernatural ability so that we may be His ambassadors.

We often think our weaknesses will stop God from using us, but the opposite is true. You see, God knows us well despite our shortcomings. God knows that if we humble ourselves and confess openly to Him, we can't do anything without Him – He will receive greater glory coming from us as weak vessels. Do you get me?

Setting Our Lives in Motion

We move because the rhythm of God moves us. If we are genuine and sincere seekers of His presence, then we will know there is a rhythm from the Lord. It is to this beat that we want to move! When setting our lives in motion, God will always lead.

As we move, God knows our human tendencies precisely. Experiencing something out of the ordinary might affect us positively or negatively. If, while following the Lord, we run into some trouble, we might become afraid and run, as with the disciples who said they would never leave or abandon Jesus. As soon as the soldiers appeared to arrest Him at the prayer garden at Gethsemane, they all fled and abandoned Him. So, God knows our hearts.

The Wisdom of God

In the story of the children of Israel coming out of Egypt, we find God's strategic mindset at work. He knew His people very well: their fears, their doubts, their complaining attitude, their stubborn hearts, etc. He knew them like no other!

Knowing their fear, God decided to bring the children of

Israel through the wilderness through the Red Sea. Specifically, the Lord outlines why He didn't take them through the shortcut, the Philistine's territory (which was much more accessible and closer). By the way, the road to life is always narrow and never easy!

God's Motive

"...for God said, "Lest perhaps the people change their minds when they see war and return to Egypt." There we have it, the motive for not going through the road of lesser resistance. God knew that if His people heard about having to fight or having any conflict in moving forward, they would return to Egypt. God wasn't going to put His people in a vulnerable position. Sometimes, God allows this, but this wasn't one of them. God knew His people were frail and traumatized – He cared for them all through.

In closing, God's leadership is always present in our lives. He knows our weaknesses and knows well that we are nothing but dust. Therefore, God leads us with wisdom beyond our years and gets us to His desired place. Neh'enah.

31

Nasa!

"And Moses said to the people, "Do not be afraid. Stand still, and see the salvation of the LORD, which He will accomplish for you today. For the Egyptians whom you see today, you shall see again no more forever. The LORD will fight for you, and you shall hold your peace." And the LORD said to Moses, "Why do you cry to Me? Tell the children of Israel to go forward. But lift up your rod, stretch out your hand over the sea, and divide it. And the children of Israel shall go on dry ground through the midst of the sea. And I indeed will harden the hearts of the Egyptians, and they shall follow them. So, I will gain honor over Pharaoh and over all his army, his chariots, and his horsemen. Then the Egyptians shall know that I am the LORD, when I have gained honor for Myself over Pharaoh, his chariots, and his horsemen." (Exodus 14:13-18)

In our walk of faith, we will always come across many obstacles. The obstacles are not placed by chance but by strategy. The Lord desires that we enter a deeper trust and a more intimate understanding of His love for us.

Too often, believers find themselves trapped by "earthly" trials and circumstances of such magnitude that they send them on a tailspin and leave them wondering if they will ever come out of this one.

Such was the story we find in Exodus 14. God was about to do one of the most amazing miracles known to man – the opening of the Red Sea. This was perhaps one of the most challenging trials for God's people. You see, the people had fled in a hurry by permission of Pharaoh to go and worship God in the desert (a long-awaited prayer of theirs.). In this, God sent them out and went before them.

What we need to know as well is this - God was going to put an end to Pharaoh's army in the process.

As God's people fled, Pharaoh changed his mind and started pursuing them. God's people were between a rock and a hard place. A desert on both sides, Pharaoh's army in hot pursuit, and the Red Sea in front. This is enough to make anyone cry! I'm sure you have been to this same place a time or two.

The Promise

"Do not be afraid. Stand still, and see the salvation of the LORD, which He will accomplish for you today. For the Egyptians whom you see today, you shall see again no more forever. The LORD will fight for you, and you shall hold your peace."

Here's one thing we must learn. The promise is just words given. Understanding a commitment intellectually doesn't mean much if our hearts are disengaged. Let me say it this way: If the words or promise are not mixed with faith, the promise will not take root and manifest! There must be a promise and faith working together to get results.

Way too often, believers get excited about a promise. They go around telling everyone how the Lord spoke to them and how that some prophet gave them a word, only not to see it come to pass. Why would this be?

It might come to pass if you hear something and take it to heart. This only happens when the word given is not appropriated by faith. The results are imminent when you blend what God says with God's faith inside you.

Challenged to *Go Forward!*

After hearing the promise and being overjoyed, the time came for God's people to walk it out. It was here where the rubber met the road!

As God's people ran in fear while Pharaoh's army pursued them, they began doubting. Here, God told Moses, **"And the LORD said to Moses, "Why do you cry to Me? Tell the children of Israel to go forward."**

NASA

Go forward in its original Hebrew comes from the word NASA, which means to pull out or up, set out, journey.

As we walk with God and position ourselves to move by faith, we must learn to rise in the Spirit of the Lord. God told Moses to tell the children to go forward – going forward means to elevate, to pull out or up, and set out on the journey. We must rise to God's dimension and flow on this spiritual road, not the earthly route of fear, doubt, and unbelief.

Nasa is taking place! Nasa is a spiritual act of faith. Nasa is a spiritual term that only applies to the spiritual man or woman. Let me encourage you that when you and I rise in the power of the Spirit, we go forward. The results will be that nothing will stop or hurt us. Neh'enah.

32

Is the Lord Among Us or Not?

"Then all the congregation of the children of Israel set out on their journey from the Wilderness of Sin, according to the commandment of the LORD, and camped in Rephidim; but there was no water for the people to drink. Therefore, the people contended with Moses and said, "Give us water, that we may drink." So, Moses asked them, "Why do you contend with me? Why do you tempt the LORD?" And the people thirsted there for water, and the people complained against Moses, and said, "Why is it you have brought us up out of Egypt, to kill us and our children and our livestock with thirst? So, Moses cried out to the LORD, saying, "What shall I do with this people? They are almost ready to stone me!" And the LORD said to Moses, "Go on before the people, and take with you some of the elders of Israel. Also take in your hand your rod with which you struck the river and go. Behold, I will stand before you there on the rock in Horeb; and you shall strike the rock, and water will come out of it, that the people may drink." And Moses did so in the sight of the elders of Israel. So, he called the name of the place Massah and Meribah, because of the contention of the children of Israel, and because they tempted the LORD, saying, "Is the LORD among us or not?" (Exodus 17:1-7)

As God moves our lives from one spiritual place to another, a profound work occurs. Too often don't see this work being done, but trust me, God works even when we think He is not!

In meditating upon His word this day, I came across this beautiful revelation in Exodus 17. It is the story where the children of Israel went to Rephidim.

Rephidim!

Rephidim was a place in the desert.

If you remember, the children of Israel, not too long before, had come out of Egyptian bondage and had made a transference from Egypt to the Wilderness of Sin and all along while being led by the commandment of the Lord.

Please notice that God's people never did call the shots or made any decisions as they came out of the house of Egyptian bondage. God led them all the way through. We often think that they thought of this significant breakthrough, and in passing through the Red Sea, they could perform this miracle. This is not the way it went down.

The way that this breaking out took place was initiated by God and maintained by God. The Lord's leadership brought them out; by His power, he opened the Red Sea so they could pass through the dry ground. It was all God!

Now the Lord had brought them to a place called Rephidim. This was a deserted place, and what better to expose our fleshly nature than an excellent hot desert?

Deserts in typology always speak of times of testing. Loneliness, abandonment, breaking, challenges, and endurance will be the topics we all deal with in a desert experience.

Exposing Our Flesh!

"Therefore, the people contended with Moses and said, "Give us water, that we may drink." So, Moses said to them, "Why do you contend with me? Why do you tempt the LORD?" And the people thirsted there for water, and the people complained against Moses, and said, "Why is it you have brought us up out of Egypt, to kill us and our children and our livestock with thirst?"

It wasn't long before God's people started to manifest what was indeed in their hearts; the awful rebellion and mean spirit that they carried within was soon to burst and manifest its ugly head!

It is incredible how fragile and fickle we are as human beings. We say one thing on Monday and change our minds on Tuesday. The promises of God are taken out of the spiritual context; because of this, we waver and usually change our course. People need more perseverance, among other things.

Seeing Our True Self!

God will allow us to go through stuff like this – all for the sake of us seeing our true selves! God's people didn't see Jehovah God as their all in all. It was good while He performed some mighty miracles; as soon as they were to make some headway through the desert, they folded.

Nothing exposes our humanness like a good dessert! Nothing will bring us to the end of ourselves like adversity.

Things got so hard that they rebelled against Moses and the Lord, saying, **"Is the Lord among us or not?"**

The Lord will always work with our character. He will lead us to places that make us grow and realize that we need Him more than we know. Until we learn that God desires us to grow, we will not see His hand at work in us.

It is time to open our eyes and lift our vision higher. It is the only way to walk in the complete joy of the Lord. Neh'enah.

33

Fire Begets Fire!

"Then the LORD said to Moses, "Come up to Me on the mountain and be there; and I will give you tablets of stone, and the law and commandments which I have written, that you may teach them." So, Moses arose with his assistant Joshua, and Moses went up to the mountain of God. And he said to the elders, "Wait here for us until we return to you. Indeed, Aaron and Hur are with you. If any man has a difficulty, let him go to them." Then Moses went up into the mountain, and a cloud covered the mountain. Now the glory of the LORD rested on Mount Sinai, and the cloud covered it six days. And on the seventh day He called to Moses out of the midst of the cloud. The sight of the glory of the LORD was like a consuming fire on the top of the mountain in the eyes of the children of Israel. So, Moses went into the midst of the cloud and went up into the mountain. And Moses was on the mountain forty days and forty nights." (Exodus 24:12-18)

The Lord told Moses, **"Come up to Me on the mountain and be there."** How would you handle these words? What would be your reaction to this invitation? Would you be overtaken with the emotion of learning personally from God, or would you be afraid of the outcome of such an encounter?

The Lord had been working with Moses for some time and felt that Moses was now ready for the next level of spiritual growth in His life. It was time to come up higher to the mountain of God and be there until the revelation came.

The Lord told Moses that He would be giving him tablets of stone with the laws and commandments so that he would teach them to His people. God was about to transform this vessel into a mighty testimony of His glory. It was a time or season in Moses' life to go deeper and climb higher than ever.

God's Cloud

The Scripture says Moses **"went up into the mountain, and a cloud covered the mountain."** Has God's cloud covered you? What does it mean to be surrounded by God's cloud? To me, God's cloud symbolizes disappearing into His purpose and plan. It might be when God shuts you down for a season so that you may seek Him wholeheartedly. A season when the servant of God is shut in with the Lord in prayer and fasting. It's not a time for information but a time for revelation, indeed!

In the cloud of God, a man must realize God's timing. God is not in a hurry, but we might be. After seeking and following God's commands for some time, Moses was about to learn to be patient with the Lord. He took him into the mountain where His glory was and made him wait there. Moses stayed for six days in this glorious experience before God talked to him on the seventh day. Here, God was about to unfold revelatory information that would impact history.

If we don't learn to be patient with the Lord, we will never receive anything from God. We must become increasingly acquainted with His timing with our need to know.

The mountain of God, Sinai, was full of the fire of God's glory. It was intense, and Moses was about to go into it.

Many have asked how I get God's fire in my life. You get God's fire by spending time in His fire! This may entail many different things to different people but see what Moses did: **"So Moses went into the midst of the cloud and went up into the mountain. And Moses was on the mountain forty days and forty nights."**

My dear friends, Moses was in the fire of God's glory for forty days and forty nights! Is it any wonder why God could work with such a man? Is it clear why God would use Moses and not Judas Iscariot?

What About My Fire?

As I close this word, let me say that if you are facing fiery trials, circumstances, or various forms of adversities – if you believe God is allowing you to go through them, it is probably because God wants to ignite your soul. You don't get anything if you don't see Jesus in any of it! It is all on the perception of who is holding the cup of pain! [see John 18:11] Neh'enah

34

Holy Delays!

"Now when the people saw that Moses delayed coming down from the mountain, the people gathered together to Aaron, and said to him, "Come, make us gods that shall go before us; for as for this Moses, the man who brought us up out of the land of Egypt, we do not know what has become of him." And Aaron said to them, "Break off the golden earrings which are in the ears of your wives, your sons, and your daughters, and bring them to me." So, everyone broke off the golden earrings in their ears and brought them to Aaron. And he received the gold from their hand, fashioned it with an engraving tool, and made a molded calf. Then they said, "This is your god, O Israel, that brought you out of the land of Egypt!" So, when Aaron saw it, he built an altar before it." (Exodus 32:1-5)

I chose to entitle this chapter of my devotional Holy Delays. Holy because almost all the delays we experience in our lifetime are initiated by the Lord for His good pleasure.

Delays differ from what we want when we need to be somewhere. Delays expose our true selves, and if we are honest about it, they also reveal our present character.

Up to this point, the Hebrew children had been led by Moses & Aaron. It appears that the people were following with a good attitude, and by the text, they were learning to see how God was working in their midst.

As it always happens with most of us, so long as things are flowing in our favor, there is no need to get upset about anything. You see, God knows that!

How can God work a little deeper in our character and develop our spirit more significantly? How can we gain spiritual authority over many areas in our lives? We might not immediately see this kind of work going on inside of us, but we will eventually see the fuller intention of the Lord for us, just like the Hebrew children did.

Moses Up on the Mountain!

The Scripture says that Moses had gone up to be with God for forty-plus days. He practically disappeared into the glory of God and was caught up with God for all these days.

Did Moses's absence make the people of God lose their way, or was it always in their hearts to follow their wayward ways? God had been faithful to them through and through; He had provided a crossing through the Red Sea, a mighty deliverance if you ask me. God had taken good care of them through His servant Moses – why would they think Moses had abandoned them? As you read on, you will discover that God's people were so full of themselves and that the only thing that mattered to them was their health and life. Selfishness at its finest! Sound a lot like the gospel that preachers teach and preach in our present day.

Creating an Option!

They created an option as they looked for Moses, and he was nowhere to be found. Here's what their fleshly selfish hearts said: **"Come, make us gods that shall go before us; for as for this Moses, the man who brought us up out of the land of Egypt, we do not know what has become of him."**

Reading this scripture, I realized that this is precisely what happens in the human heart that doesn't intimately know God. The soul that is not surrendered to the Holy Spirit has the unstoppable and unquenchable tendency to rebel and go against all that God has set for us not to do.

Though someone may appear righteous, pious, and humble, it doesn't mean that they indeed are. It may all be a facade. They may only be masquerading as Christians, but truthfully, they are in name only! These so-called servants of God have an external reputation but have never been intimate with God!

The Real Test

The real test for all believers comes when God is testing them. The test challenges the person in attitude, commitment, loyalty, decision-making, faithfulness, and character. These tests are given with the sole purpose of exposing the natural person.

As the great Apostle and founder of the Vineyard movement once said, *God will offend the mind to reveal the heart.*

God will always look for opportunities to bring us to a place where we learn how different we are from Him and, through His Spirit, will help us conform to His image. Neh'enah.

35

Awake & Conscious in God's Presence!

"For we do not wrestle against flesh and blood, but against principalities, against powers, against the rulers of the darkness of this age, against spiritual hosts of wickedness in the heavenly places." (Ephesians 6:12)

The fact that you and I have been born-again by the Spirit of God and through faith we have been lifted with Christ and are seated in heavenly places doesn't guarantee that all battles are over and done with.

The battle for possessing spiritual territory has begun, and to take Paul's words to heart when he said, **"I can do all things through Christ who strengthens me,"** is a pivotal point in how we look at life now.

Through Christ, we fight our warfare; through Christ, we advance in spiritual power; yes, it is through Christ that we possess all the territory that God has freely given us. Only through Christ can we stand against the wiles of the enemy!

Do You Believe it?

Too often, I hear believers make affirmations, confessions,

or decrees that they don't believe in their hearts. For the most part, young believers tend to parakeet others. Just because someone had the victory over a particular situation doesn't mean you will have success in your case.

We must allow God to dominate our hearts and possess us in every area of our lives before we can genuinely advance and be people who walk in spiritual authority.

In the Scripture of Ephesians 6:12, I find that our war is genuinely spiritual, making us vulnerable in the fight if we can't discern the enemy's schemes. Paul says our battle is **"against spiritual hosts of wickedness in the heavenly places."** If you are an individual who tends to get full of himself or is arrogant and proud, the enemy will have you for lunch.

You see, it doesn't matter how big, how spiritual, or how well-versed we might think we are; if pride is in our hearts, it will be the devil's magnet to attract him and give him enough of the foothold needed to put is in bondage and eventually silence our lives.

The Early Morning Ant!

On one of my morning jogs, after I had finished my run, I was stretching before heading home. While I tried, I noticed an ant walking by my feet, going about its business. For some ought to reason, it caught my attention. I saw it and pondered how little she was and how big my foot was next to it. I thought, "I can step on it and demolish it to powder if necessary. I am bigger and stronger and heavier!" Right after this thought, the Lord said, *This is how I see the enemy of your soul, like a little ant.*

As I meditated upon these words, the Spirit of the Lord quickened me and said to me, *"When you are awake and conscious in My presence David, this is how life will always be for you. You are invincible! Nothing can touch you. But when you fall asleep and become unconscious to My presence, even this little ant can climb on you and bite you! So, it is never on how big the ant (or problem) is; the issue will always be, "are we awake and conscious in His presence?"*

Let me say that our warfare will entail much more than just ordinary praying and Bible reading; it will take a more concerted effort from us and a more intentional approach to stay awake and conscious of His presence every day! Then and only then will we advance and possess our rightful territory!

Your Spiritual Slumber Will Hurt You!

"Now, two women who were harlots came to the king and stood before him. And one woman said, "O my lord, this woman and I dwell in the same house; and I gave birth while she was there. Then it happened, the third day after I had given birth, that this woman also gave birth. And we were together; no one was with us in the house, except the two of us in the house. And this woman's son died in the night because she lay on him. So, she arose in the middle of the night and took my son from my side, while your maidservant slept, and laid him in her bosom, and laid her dead child in my bosom. And when I rose in the morning to nurse my son, there he was, dead. But when I had examined him in the morning, indeed, he was not my son whom I had borne." (1 Kings 3:16-21)

In the passage of 1 Kings 3:16-21, we find the story of two harlots who lived in the same house. One of the women (first harlot) had a baby; three days later, the other (second) also had a baby.

In the morning, the first harlot recognized that the baby who was dead was not hers. As the (second) harlot slept, she laid on her baby and killed it. She then went and took the first harlot's baby and exchanged it for her dead baby while the first harlot slept.

Please notice that the second harlot fell asleep and killed her valuable possession; the first harlot also fell asleep, but she gathered herself and recognized that the dead baby was not hers.

These two examples teach us that we can't afford to fall asleep, or we will kill what is valuable; now, if we do fall asleep, we better wake up to recognize what is of God and what is not.

Some too many people are in the church today but unconscious of God's presence and all He is doing in them. It is time to wake up and take all God has given us!

Neh'enah.

36

With Everything in You, Walk in Forgiveness!

"And whenever you stand praying, if you have anything against anyone, forgive him, that your Father in heaven may also forgive you your trespasses. But if you do not forgive, neither will your heavenly Father forgive your trespasses." (Mark 11:25-27)

Meditating this morning on this one set of Scriptures, the Holy Spirit brought the subject of forgiveness to my mind. You must remember that when you read the Word of God and a truth pops up before you, it could mean that the Holy Spirit wants to talk to you about the subject at hand.

This subject has so much power that if anyone dares to believe its truth, it can free them from things that continue to plague them and eventually destroy them.

Nothing kills one's emotional, spiritual, and eventually physical life like the sin of unforgiveness and a bitter heart. My friends, listen, there is only one remedy to overcome this evil force. What am I talking about? I'm talking about good old-fashioned forgiveness!

In walking with God all these years, I have understood

the power of forgiveness in a small way. I learned how it freed me when I was held in bondage by the guilt and shame of sin, and I also experienced the release when I forgave those who offended me.

Too often, those who have been affected by the offenses of others struggle to forgive. It is not easy to do it – especially when you were assaulted, attacked, or robbed of something valuable.

We are called to love everyone – enemies especially! When others have ripped us off, we demand a payback, a restitution of all that was taken from us; and I do get the thinking behind it. Yet, there is a more profound law in God: the law of love.

It is hard to hate or be critical of someone when you have prayed for them. It is challenging to slander or gossip about any individual when you have forgiven them from your heart.

Jesus gives us something to consider here in these verses. Check this out.

What is Forgiveness from God's Point of View

The word to forgive in Greek means "to send off" or "to hurl" (e.g., missiles) to "to release," "to let go," or "to let be." Listen to its original meaning – it is saying something profound here.

In forgiving any offense, one is to "send it off!" In the picture, you are packaging your violation in a box and mailing it away from you. How about the words "to hurl," like a missile? Do you see how badly Jesus wants us to understand the value of forgiveness? It is almost as if Jesus essentially says, "I don't want you to allow any unforgiveness to have dominion over you. Please get rid of it and get rid of it now. Hurl it like a missile away from you!" Note: hurling depicts force and intent! Jesus is saying, "Unforgiveness is a trap! It intends to trap you behind a cell block and hold you back in life. Don't allow this trap to get you: send it off, release it, let go, and just let it be!"

The Contingency

In forgiving someone for an offense, you must also remember that your forgiveness is on hold until you forgive those who have trespassed against you. You will not find forgiveness for your sins unless you forgive the other person from your heart!

Yes, our forgiveness is contingent upon our forgiving of other sins against us. **"But if you do not forgive, neither will your Father in heaven forgive your trespasses."** Neh'enah.

37

Marked by a Promise!

"Now Israel loved Joseph more than all his children because he was the son of his old age. Also, he made him a tunic of many colors. But when his brothers saw that their father loved him more than all his brothers, they hated him and could not speak peaceably to him." (Genesis 37:3, 4)

"When He had been baptized, Jesus came up immediately from the water; and behold, the heavens were opened to Him, and He saw the Spirit of God descending like a dove and alighting upon Him. And suddenly a voice came from heaven, saying, "This is My beloved Son, in whom I am well pleased." (Matthew 3:16, 17)

In my prayer time today, God brought this set of events to my attention. Though in different time slots, the revelation that God gave me regarding these two events deals with the promises given by God, killed by God, and resurrected by God.

As I have pursued the heart of the Lord, I have come to realize how God works in us and breaks us; yes, all for the sake of us attaining a more excellent knowledge, not only OF Him but IN Him.

There is no other way to get a greater revelation of who Christ is unless one is brought into a life of brokenness and a greater longing for His heart.

One of the things you might have experienced in your own life might be with a promise God made to you. As the Lord walks through with us a promise He made to us personally, He will also kill that promise before our eyes!

I'm sure you have experienced disappointments, especially when the Lord led you to a challenging place, and you were convinced that God would bless you in some way, only to discover that nothing happened! To top it off, things only got worse and worse from then on, and there was nothing you could do about it! Does this sound familiar to you?

But God, You Said…

Many of us have been to this place at one time or another. How often have we quoted a promise, a decree, a prophetic word given to us by someone, or even a prophetic dream – all to no avail? God made a promise, but nothing has happened… at least not yet or not here on earth.

From God's point of view, we must understand that when He makes a promise, He sets everything that involves that promise in motion. So, please know that the promise is about you and those around you.

Often people think that God is like Santa Claus - waiting for our wish list so that he may give us all the toys we want. This form of thinking needs to be revised! One thing to always keep in mind as we develop this excellent walk with God is that the Lord is more concerned about our spiritual maturity and growth.

Loved More!

In the case of Joseph, his father, Jacob, loved him more than all his other children. This wasn't by mistake but by design – the design of God. Is it any wonder why the other brothers were jealous of Joseph? You know the answer to that.

Jacob loved Joseph more than all his children and made it clear by giving him a coat of many colors as if continual praise of him wasn't enough. This made all the siblings upset, not to mention envious.

God's gift marked Joseph upon Him. The coat of many colors speaks of favor and blessing. But I also believe Joseph was kept for you and me to see and recognize the life of a man that the Lord chooses.

When God shows favor to us, it also sends a loud declaration of blessing to all who know us. The word is loud and clear, and there is no mistaking the message: God is for you! In this case, it would be Joseph, the favored one.

God marked him, and God himself would be with him through all the trials of his life.

I am convinced that the Lord gives us a glimpse of a promising future and reveals to us what He wants to accomplish in us and through us, but that won't happen without us first being severely tested.

People Look at the Outside of a Man!

People are always enamored with the external; too few understand the inner life and what it means to walk with God. People who walk with God know that the coat of many colors only symbolizes a life God has marked.

God can make a showcase of these servants. He can make promises to them; He can take the pledge away; He can resurrect it once again; and He can make the pledge manifest even in unfavorable conditions! It is this type of man or woman that God can trust to a greater degree, if you will.

When God finds a man or woman that He can trust, He can do His will through them by displaying them. When a man has come out of a harsh season of pain and struggle, the glory on their face is priceless, and their spirit is like an unquenchable fire!

In this same pattern, Jesus, the Son of God, our King, was

displayed for all to see. His virgin birth, the life of suffering and resurrection, was to bring God glory!

Was it easy for Jesus to walk in His Father's will? I think not. You see, we walk with God because we love Him, we obey Him because He is worthy, and we never walk with God because of convenience or to see what we get from Him!

You must know that Jesus walked with God because He wanted to honor the Father with pure obedience, not because it was easy. Yet in all His suffering, He saw something different than you, and I would see. Listen to this: "…[Jesus] **who for the joy that was set before him endured the cross, despising the shame, and is seated at the right hand of the throne of God.**" (Hebrews 12:2)

In closing, I have come to learn a few things in the Spirit of the Lord. One of them is that God will give us a promise either by clothing us with favor or speaking words of affirmation to us, but by the same token, He will also take us to the place of brokenness. This is where we get to die to all our ambitions and dreams to live the life He desires. We must always know that He will resurrect any vision, plan, or promise He has made to us in His timing! Neh'enah.

38

Betraying Emotions!

"And when they had sung a hymn, they went out to the Mount of Olives.
Then Jesus said to them, "All of you will be made to stumble because of Me this night, for it is written:
'I will strike the Shepherd,
And the sheep of the flock will be scattered.'
But after I have been raised, I will go before you to Galilee."
Peter answered and said to Him, "Even if all are made to stumble because of You, I will never be made to stumble."
Jesus said to him, "Assuredly, I say to you that this night, before the rooster crows, you will deny Me three times."
Peter said to Him, "Even if I have to die with You, I will not deny You!"
And so said all the disciples." (Matthew 26:30-35)

I can't recall, or will even attempt to do so, of the countless times I have betrayed my emotions, though, when making a promise, I was so sure and convinced that what I promised I would be able to keep!

We have all been here at this place: breaking other people's hearts because of our lack of ability to do what we said we would do—not keeping our promises, not fulfilling what was expected from us, or simply not keeping honoring vows. Do you know what I am talking about? I'm sure you do.

Emotions Are Not Enough!

Let me begin my devotion by saying emotions are as strong as vapor. I'm not trying to be sarcastic, but isn't it true that our feelings come and go like the wind? One day you feel good; another day, you can feel terrible. One day you feel full of strength, only to find the next day full of depression and an inability to overcome.

I don't claim to be an authority on the subject or even hold a degree in psychology, but I know that I, like Peter, have made vows and promises that I failed miserably (to be honest) and was unable to keep!

When vows and promises are made when the emotions are high, one will always run the danger of falling on their face by not keeping what was said. Peter was on a high and thus spoke what he felt, not what he knew. Too often, this is precisely what we all go through – we get excited about the possibilities but don't consider the cost. I'm not saying it is terrible, but how often have we fallen into this trap?

How Do We Overcome Emotional Rushes?

I have learned a few things along the way about overcoming emotional rushes. Let me share with you a few secrets from my experience:

When the emotions are high, let us first count the cost.

Knowing that emotions will run dry soon [and we must understand this fact], we must count the cost first and then figure out what we will be left with [I'm speaking of the responsibility, commitment, resources, etc.] after the emotions are gone. Once the dreaming is done, we are left with reality. Can we turn the dream into reality?

Will we be able to finish what we start? We must know this before we start.

You see, our emotions will get it started, but our minds will keep it going. How robust is our thought process as we venture out? If we can't see ourselves finishing the project, let it be a sign that we should not get started. One must be able to build something twice: once in our mind and the other in real life!

As we learned from Peter (being on an emotionally high attitude), he told Jesus that he would never abandon Him. Peter operated out of his emotion, not his thought process. Consequently, Peter failed miserably and negated that he knew Jesus at all. Is there anything more heartbreaking than that?

You see, emotions are good when set in motion by the Lord. The Spirit of the Lord will carry us through any process He initiates. But we must also know that if the Holy Spirit is not the One moving our hearts, we will burn out quickly and fail in our promise. Neh'enah.

Volume 7

39

Finishing Well!

"**And those who had laid hold of Jesus led Him away to Caiaphas the high priest, where the scribes and the elders were assembled. But Peter followed Him at a distance to the high priest's courtyard. And he went in and sat with the servants to see the end.**" (Matthew 26:57-58)

Growing up in competition and developing different skills playing either football, basketball, or chess, the winner usually has the best talent, consistent discipline, and a persevering heart. If one can apply these three elements to anything, one will get used to winning almost always.

A person can have a great idea and start it with hardly any problem. The wind of emotion and excitement is there, and it can usually carry you for about 90% of the time until the uphill climb begins! This usually happens on the last round, with only 15 minutes left on the clock of life for accomplishing any endeavor. I'm not saying the Lord told me to say this; I have just had a lot of birthdays and failures to know that this is true!

Peter the Apostle

Now, let me illustrate from the word of God how this principle applies. Peter was a fisherman, and Jesus recruited people with skill, discipline, and perseverance. Peter qualified himself by being a fisherman. Jesus handpicked him.

Peter had the best seat in the house, meaning he was handpicked by Jesus and had been given precious promises. He was that special to Jesus. One thing to note here is that Jesus knew that Peter was not perfect and needed much work in his character. This goes for all of us – trust me, He knows us well!

Peter was a hands-on type of guy. He didn't wait for things to materialize; he would make things happen. Thus, his impatient character and tendency to falter in attitude and godly wisdom.

From what I read in the Scriptures, Peter seemed to have the edge over the other eleven apostles. He carried himself with an attitude as if he was God's answer for humanity type of person. He knew it all, and he did it all.

A Day in a Life!

As it usually happens to all of us when God is getting ready to use our lives, He will put us inside a furnace of testing; yes, Peter was about to enter his furnace!

While making all these promises to Jesus, Peter vowed

never to abandon Him. Jesus knew better and told him exactly what would happen.

Peter was to be tested in the most challenging lesson– his loyalty to Christ!

The Season is Here!

I see three things happening while we enter a season of testing. Let me share them with you.

The first step in the testing furnace is this; God will call us to follow Him with singleness of heart. He wants all of us, not just 95%. He wants 100% of us! This is God's aim, vision, and mission to accomplish in us – a 100% devotion to Him. This is the first step in the furnace of testing.

We will face all kinds of challenges and adversities. Usually, these challenges will be more significant than ours. We cannot deal with them in the power of our flesh. It will take a more profound revelation of Christ to find our way out of these challenges. Peter was prepared for this.

The second step in the testing furnace is when failure to pass the first step grips us. Our attitude toward accomplishing the goal starts to wane. We get weaker, rebellious, and in many cases, defiant; yet, we still follow, but from a distance.

You see, Peter took off when they arrested Jesus in the garden. He didn't know what to do. He couldn't understand why Jesus told him to remove his sword after cutting the soldier's ear. It was a different type of war; Peter didn't know it!

So first, we are called to enter a deeper walk with Christ, and that decision will be tested. Then, we are challenged to stick around, but we don't, at least not hand in hand with Jesus, but from a distance.

Finally, the furnace of testing will challenge us to press in, but too often, people give up and end up sitting on the stands. The Scripture says that Peter followed from a distance, and when he came into the priest's court, he went in and sat with the servants to see how the game would end.

How does one go from being a player on the field to a fan in the stands?

Please understand that God will test every decision you make of allegiance to Him. He will bring adversity to test your character; He will bring you to a place of significant failure so that He may help you understand His heart.

When all these things begin to happen, don't panic. The point is to finish well – in the center of God's purpose for your life! Ask God to lead you by His Spirit and bring you to a greater revelation of Christ Himself. Neh'enah.

40

Soldiers of the Cross of Christ!

"You, therefore, my son, be strong in the grace of Christ Jesus. And the things that you have heard from me among many witnesses, commit these to faithful men who can teach others also. You therefore must endure hardship as a good soldier of Jesus Christ. No one engaged in warfare entangles himself with the affairs of this life, that he may please him who enlisted him as a soldier." (2 Timothy 4:1-5)

Nothing shakes a person's inward core more than knowing that you might be going to war and have to fight to defend your country. When people discover their nation is about to go through a possible war, they either run to it or away from it.

I'm sure every individual will begin to count the cost; some will understand that their life and family might be affected forever! Things will be different and never return to being the same way things presently are.

I have seen that in the kingdom of God, believers tend to do the same. Many runs to the war and others run away from it.

How are these attitudes formed? Where do they come from? I have a theory to all this and one that I have come to develop over many years of serving God through thick and thin on the battlefield of life.

Prospered to Death!

Most people who live in the western world think that America is heaven. That everyone else in the world needs to have what we have. For example, many believers feel that we should all be blessed (which means wealth and health and a few toys on the side.)

Most western Christians equate blessings with good things. We have made idols of these materialistic blessings and have settled as far as our spiritual growth is concerned. With this mindset, we don't pursue the things that matter to the heart of God (i.e., His perfect will, what He wants or expects from me, dealing with my sins and rebellion, etc.) We become more concerned with our worldview (my life, pain, job, marriage, etc.)

Hardships of a Soldier

Hardships of a soldier begin with a life of discipline. Walking out your Christianity is not just coming to church on time – it is way more than that. Fields that affect your life are not fun. They are painful. *An experience of God that doesn't cost you nothing doesn't do nothing!*, said Leonard

Ravenhill.

Personal prayer is one of the most challenging disciplines to keep daily. Most preachers can't even pray 15 minutes a day! Can you imagine their congregations? Meeting God daily will help us develop an intimate life with God.

The intake of God's word must be on your to-do list for this new year. Without the word of God as a central pillar that holds you up, you have no chance of survival in this spiritual world. You cannot be a true soldier of Jesus and not be submitted to the Word of God.

Regular fasting is also one of those disciplines that will help us overcome many personal battles of the mind and heart. Choosing God over food will not be easy, but it will be the most rewarding.

Finally, being quick to hear and obey will be the attitude that makes you a soldier. Those who don't understand this or do but choose not to honor this rule are walking casualties. They won't be around for long!

Entangled!

In closing, let me show you what happens with those who run around entangled with the world.

In the text above, Paul said not to do it: **"No one engaged**

in warfare entangles himself with the affairs of this life...." What does an entangled person look like? The word entangled means to weave in, to entwine, i.e., to involve with. Also, to become involved in some task or role to the point that it interferes with other activities; is conceived of as being or becoming intertwined in a line to the end of immobility.

If you are entangled with the world, let me tell you something: **"Be sure your sin will find you out!"** (Numbers 32:23) As all sins, little by little, it will entangle us and will trap us to the point where we won't be able to carry out or please the One who enlisted us.

Let us walk in the power of this calling. Let us learn to please Christ with our whole being. Not only when things are going well but even when things are going wrong. Neh'enah

41

It's About the Journey!

"Then the LORD spoke to Moses, saying, "Speak to the children of Israel, and say to them: 'I am the LORD your God. According to the doings of the land of Egypt, where you dwelt, you shall not do; and according to the doings of the land of Canaan, where I am bringing you, you shall not do; nor shall you walk in their ordinances. You shall observe My judgments and keep My ordinances, to walk in them: I am the LORD your God. You shall therefore keep My statutes and My judgments, which if a man does, he shall live by them: I am the Lord." (Leviticus 18:1-5)

Don't Follow the Old Patterns from Egypt!

When the people of God lived in Egypt, it wasn't for a few weeks or months; they lived there for over 400 years. It is only natural that in that period, they would eventually learn the ways of the Egyptians.

Their customs and religious practices were some of the things that were most easy to follow. The people of God never lacked food, clothing, housing, work, and a place and time to worship Jehovah. Yet, in all this, God told them not to practice any customs or styles of worship or objects of worship done in Egypt. I am sure this wasn't easy to let go of because they had been embedded in a culture full of false gods. To all this, Moses reminded God's people not to practice.

It is the same with you and me today – when we left the world (Egypt), we were called to leave all the old practices behind. Our sinful lifestyle, ungodly friends and relationships, religious beliefs regarding how we worship God, etc.

Don't Follow the Present Patterns from Canaan!

As Moses continued teaching God's people, he added that they should not learn the ways of the Canaanites either. These tribes were found in the new place they were headed to. These tribes were found in the Promised Land, and Moses warned them not to learn their ways. He told them, **"...nor shall you walk in their ordinances."**

Reading and meditating upon these verses, I realized that following God is not about where we have been or are going!

Most people tend to have the understanding that we are to leave the world for a better world. Though this sounds theologically correct, it is deeper and more intricate than that thought. Let me explain.

We are called to Observe God!

"You shall observe My judgments and keep My ordinances, to walk in them: I am the LORD your God. You shall therefore keep My statutes and My judgments, which if a man does, he shall live by them: I am the Lord."

I can understand leaving Egypt as a follower of Jehovah God, but if He is taking me out of something wicked – wouldn't it be correct to say He is now bringing me into something new, something promising? This is partially true.

You see, God brings us out of Egypt (the world) so we can be free to worship Him alone. So apparently, by the text, God is getting them to a land that flows with milk and honey, a Promised Land; this would be Canaan's land.

Moses quickly then notes: When you come to Canaan, you are not to learn their ways either. We leave one world (Egypt) to go to another (Canaan) but are not allowed to learn their ways. So, what is it?

Here's what I got...

The Lord is interested in bringing us out of Egypt; He is also interested in our spiritual growth in Canaan, the land of promise. Now, the Promised Land is a destination for those who have learned the ways of the Lord in the wilderness.

You can't enjoy the Promised Land unless you have learned God's judgments, ordinances, and statutes in the journey! It is not about where we have been or where we are headed. It is about walking with Him daily on the journey of life. It is about learning His ways in the journey! Are you getting this?

Too often, we have looked for a sign from heaven, a prophetic word to keep us flowing in our daily life, a promise that things will be all right, or even for God to give us a dream or vision assuring us that the future is bright.

Let me tell you something: There is no need for any of these, although all the different things I mentioned do happen. I am saying that as we journey with God, we learn the ways of the Spirit of God, learn His words, and learn to discern His patterns. This is the will of God for all His servants. Neh'enah

42

Stony Ground, Stony Hearts!

"Some fell on stony ground, where it did not have much earth, and immediately it sprang up because it had no depth of earth. But when the sun was up, it was scorched, withered away because it had no root." (Mark 4:5, 6)

While meditating this early morning, I came across this one portion of Scripture that started deep into my soul, and I couldn't shake it off. I spent some time praying and asking God what manner of truth this was.

The Spirit made me feel His heart on this matter and showed me how too many believers haven't disengaged from their present world and have made the conscious and willing choice not to love the things of the world and cut off all earthly attachments regarding self and sin.

I asked the Lord, "Why do we see in the Christian ministry so much backsliding, rebellion towards authority, and unproductive lives for God?"

Let me share with you what I believe the Holy Spirit began to show me, and you judge in your heart.

Not Much Earth!

For starters, most believers don't have it made, as one would say. To say that life is easy because Jesus is in our hearts is nothing more and nothing less than hype.

When people are boisterous and tend to be extreme in their devotion to Jesus, it shows me something – they don't have much depth in their lives! You may disagree with my assessment, but let me say that emotions don't have the power to keep anyone steady for an extended amount of time. It is the same as saying, if you build upon the sand, you are no more than a fool!

So-called believers who like to have spiritual pep rallies, wear Christian t-shirts and caps, and have colorful bumper stickers in their cars, which shows allegiance to Christ, are overly emotional in their commitment to Jesus. Listen: A fire doesn't need advertisement! Emotions are neutral feelings that come and go with changing times and events. Always remember, emotions alone will never be able to sustain anyone!

When the Spirit of God comes into a man or a woman, it has a certain tranquility. This tranquility is so profound that it is hard to contain within; therefore, you begin to see this glory permeate through the believer's life as if the very charisma of God is being expressed through a human vessel. It is not how loud you shout but how much glory you carry within.

"Not much earth..." as the Scripture depicts, is a picture of shallowness. People who are emotionally driven, for the most part, are shallow. They will be tested, and as Jesus said: **"But all her children justify wisdom."** (Luke 7:35). When the test comes their way, will they survive?

Immediate Apparent Results!

The Scripture goes on to say that the seed that fell on stony ground "...immediately sprang up because it had no depth of earth." How can this be? No earth, and it still sprung up?

I have known people throughout my life (not only believers) who appeared to have overnight success in their lives, business, and ministries, and I would think to myself, "Man, how can this be? I have been toiling for years and still can't see anything significant! It is not fair!" I would say to myself, of course.

It seemed like a great story until the sun came out on them....

Did I wish for someone's failure? Of course not. The reason for failure was embedded in the principle outlined in Mark 4:5, six, which says, "Stony ground is shallow, and the seeds that fall into it will spring quickly and die quickly."

But the Sun...

People who fail to see this principle at work always end up never arriving at their desired end because of shallowness. People are always looking for the next "high," the next event, to keep their spirits soaring! These people never settle anywhere on anything. Why is this? Because their hearts are unsettled from the core! They are not content with their experience in God...why not? Because they have never had fundamental knowledge based on truth. It was only at the emotional level.

The test that comes in their lives, or as the Scripture shows, **"But when the sun was up it was scorched,"** teaches you and me that the life of that seed buried on the very shallow ground will soon wither away as it is being scorched by the sun. The fire of God will burn our emotions. The flesh cannot enter God's presence! Do you understand me?

No Root, No Fruit!

Finally, the person riding high on their emotions will be disappointed and feel betrayed by their feelings. The setting of high expectations (birthed in the flesh) will come crumbling down, and the realization of the truth that says, **"...because it had no root, it withered away,"** will become natural to them.

It is at this place that the believer will have an opportunity to repent of their fleshly ways and emotionalism in thinking that God is this and that, and they will get frustrated with their lives, their bad choices, and get bitter at their circumstances, a man, and finally get mad at God.

Meditate on this: **"Those who cling to worthless idols forfeit the grace that could be theirs."** (Jonah 2:7) Neh'enah.

43

Visiting Heaven!

"After these things, I looked, and behold, a door standing open in heaven. And the first voice which I heard was like a trumpet speaking with me, saying, "Come up here, and I will show you things which must take place after this." (Revelation 4:1)

On January 21, 2023, on the 21st day of a 40-day fast, the Holy Spirit took me to heaven and showed me some exciting things I would love to share with you during this meditation.

It was around 5 am that I had a short dream of this man (whom I know personally) and his grandchildren playing at a church. They were the worship team at this ministry or church. They were on stage, and I was by the side of the stage, taking notice of their ministry in song. As I watched this worship team finish their music, the dream ended. One thing to note: no one from the family is serving the Lord presently that I know of - so this could have been a prophetic dream in nature.

Then it all began...

I was taken to heaven; I don't know how I got there. All I

know is that I was in heaven, and to verify that I was there, the Lord sent me an individual servant of God whom I knew very well; her name was Irma Navarro. She was a lady I had disciplined and mentored in my ministry on and off through the years. She passed away last year on February 2022 at the age of 75. She was a fantastic servant of God if I had ever seen one.

Now this remarkable servant of God was to be my tutor in heaven.

Let me outline what I saw, the questions I asked her, and what she revealed to me while we stood in the kingdom of God.

At first, when I saw her, I remember being so glad to see her again. She looked around 50 years old and was full of life with a beautiful bright countenance. I told her that I was so glad to see her. She welcomed me with a beautiful smile and kindness. She didn't ask me what I was doing there or anything of that nature. She received me and answered my questions as I was intrigued by my visit to God's kingdom.

I asked her, "Did you know your son-in-law passed away three years ago? Also, one of your grandchildren passed away last year – did you know, and have you seen them?" She said, "There are millions upon millions of people here, so no, I haven't seen them." It almost seemed she could not ask or inquire about life on earth. This I did notice.

I asked her, "Why is there so much traffic here?" She said, "The people are heading to work on the task that Jesus has given them." I noticed that the highways were so crowded with cars going to work. It was like Houston, Texas, during the morning rush hour. I thought to myself that many people were moving on that highway.

Then I asked her, "Where is Jesus? I want to meet Him face to face." She said, You have entered Jesus! When you stepped into heaven, you stepped into eternity. Jesus is an eternity! The kingdom of God is not only a place but also a place you step into. She said, "Jesus embodies the whole kingdom! He is the sun, the moon, the stars, and the currency in His kingdom." She continued to educate me about life in the kingdom and said, "Jesus is the King, and He decrees, and we follow." When my friend said this, I remembered the Scripture, **"These are those who did not defile themselves with women, for they remained virgins. They follow the Lamb wherever he goes. They were purchased from among humanity and offered as first fruits to God and the Lamb."** (Revelation 14:4)

My friend also told me that to the degree that one is faithful on earth, one would be placed in heaven, almost as if to say that life on earth is used for practicing the principles that we will be living in His heavenly kingdom. She said, "If you are faithful on earth, you will be put in charge of something much greater here." These words also reminded me of the Scripture that says, **"So he who had received five talents came and brought five other talents, saying, 'Lord, you delivered to me five talents; look, I have gained five more talents besides them.' His lord said, 'Well done, good and faithful servant; you were faithful over a few things; I will make you ruler over many things. Enter into the joy of your lord.'** (Matthew 25:20-21)

As this visit was almost ending, I heard the Lord say to me, "I brought you up here to show you My infrastructure – the infrastructure of My kingdom." It almost seems like the Lord wanted me to see the workings of His kingdom in heaven. The visit ended.

I don't know why this visit occurred; I only know that God brought me there. The reason will be more apparent as I continue my walk with Him here on earth.

I wrote this with great fear that I would fail to misrepresent what I saw; may the Lord's mercy go before me as this is published. All the glory to my King – the Author and Finisher of my faith!

Neh'enah.

44

Some Went & Some Were Sent!

"And He called the twelve to Himself and sent them out two by two, giving them power over unclean spirits. So, they went out and preached that people should repent. And they cast out many demons, anointed with oil many who were sick, and healed them." (Mark 6:7, 12, 13)

In the ministry of the Lord, one must realize that serving God begins with a personal encounter with Him. There must be an impartation from the Lord before one can go and do the work of God.

Let me explain this: When the disciples of Jesus met Him at first, they were invited to come and be with Him. They were introduced to a whole set of ideas, especially on what to do with the power or anointing Jesus had deposited upon them. It was here where the instruction to follow Him began.

Called to Be with Him!

In our walk with Jesus, we will constantly be challenged to humble ourselves and seek His face. This is always a challenging thing to do. People are too busy or too bright and talented; (and with some sarcasm added); it almost seems that they don't need the Holy Spirit to lead them anymore! Seeking the face of God for instruction has nearly become a lost art.

In following God's orders, one can follow the Scriptures and obey them to the letter. Many do this. Is there something wrong with this? I think there is, in a way.

The Manifest Presence of God

In my experience with God, I have lived this kind of Christianity. I know what it is to obey the word of the Lord as it is written, and I also have learned to obey God's prophetic word as it became rhema to me.

The rhema word of God has a particular element to it. The rhema word brings a specific timing and urgency to the human spirit. It quickens it to act with faith. The reality of God being present is not just a mere emotion but can be felt by people who are ministered to.

When one moves with God's timing, His presence might be felt. Not only does the person ministering feel it, but those being ministered to feel it!

There is a difference between those who move by the letter and a considerable difference between those who drive by the Spirit. The difference is that in one, there is intellect, and in the other, there is the power that can be felt!

Once the disciples had spent time with God, Jesus commissioned them to go and do miracles. If they had not been called to be with Christ, these disciples would have only an idea of what they needed to do, not a commission. There is a difference.

Some Went, and Some were Sent!

I don't know if God would be pleased with this style of service, but one thing I know: The sent people have God's backing. In the kingdom of God, many do what they feel. They get a certain feeling and move on it; would this be acceptable to God?

By back, I mean they have God's resources, anointing, favor, and clear direction to get the job done!

Knowing this, I would rather wait upon Him until He releases me to go and do what is in His heart and not in my empty head!

In closing this devotion, let me add that too many believers have gotten accustomed to someone else leading, and they follow. Are you one of those who follow? The next phase in your life might be challenging you in more profound ways; it might be time for you to seek His face for specific instructions.

If you are one of those who follow, let me challenge you

today. You will be surprised how God wants to visit you and empower your life to take care of this unfinished business! Take time to seek the Lord for those complicated and unclear situations in your personal life; let God speak to you regarding these personal battles. Neh'enah.

45

Courage!

"There was a man sent from God, whose name was John." (John 1:6)

"Now, this is the testimony of John, when the Jews sent priests and Levites from Jerusalem to ask him, "Who are you?"
He confessed, and did not deny, but confessed, "I am not the Christ."
And they asked him, "What then? Are you Elijah?"
He said, "I am not."
"Are you the Prophet?"
And he answered, "No."
Then they said to him, "Who are you, that we may give an answer to those who sent us? What do you say about yourself?"
He said: "I am
'The voice of one crying in the wilderness:
"Make straight the way of the LORD," '(John 1:19-23)

"...for Herod feared John, knowing that he was a just and holy man, and he protected him. And when he heard him, he did many things, and heard him gladly." (Mark 6:20)

When I think of the word courage, John the Baptist always comes to mind. His courage to live a life entirely to the glory of God must be one of the most amazing stories ever recorded in history.

In my quiet time today, I came across these passages that moved my heart in my devotion to God. It is not enough to just be saved; it is not enough to say that you're a child of God and that you experience good things from God. It is not enough to say that God spoke to your heart at the service, that you had a dream, or that someone spoke some remarkable positive things about your life.

Our experience with God must go beyond our personal experiences and powerfully affect the world around us! You see, Christ died for you and me. For what reason? God has called us, the church, to make a difference in people's lives and transform our culture with His power! So that we may be light in a dark world. So that we may shine so bright that darkness flees. So that we can release God's power through our hands and make a difference in society.

God's Revelation to Joshua

The Lord told Joshua, **"Only be strong and very courageous, that you may observe to do according to all the law which Moses My servant commanded you; do not turn from it to the right hand or to the left, that you may**

prosper wherever you go." (Joshua 1:7)

I dare to believe that one day while in prayer and God's Word, John the Baptist came across this passage, which revolutionized his life and didn't allow him to have an ordinary life.

I can imagine him meditating over and over the words, "Only be strong and very courageous, that you may observe to do according to all the law which Moses, My servant, commanded you!"

The word "be strong" in Hebrew means to be or grow the firm. The call of any servant of God must first begin with the idea that he must be strong if he is ever to position himself in God's divine order. This is not easy to do. If it were, everybody would do it.

Bringing your flesh under subjection must be the most challenging thing if you attempt to change your life in your strength. This is impossible to do! Courage begins in your private life first. You work on aligning your emotions, feelings, and desires with God's! If you can do this, you move on to fulfill God's orders.

God also told Joshua, **"... be very courageous."** Here it is. **Courage** here in its original Hebrew means *"to be stout, strong, bold, alert."* Let me say that to be courageous is genuinely something within the human heart inspired by faith (knowing in your heart and having the assurance and confidence) that God wants you to move or carry it out!

I believe God gives us vision so that we may do His work. This vision is imparted to us by faith. It is this faith that makes us do things that seem impossible.

John Was Fearless!

In returning to the life of John the Baptist, this man was a man of strength and courage. He wasn't presenting himself to people during his days to entertain them. He wasn't presenting himself to religious leaders to have a spiritual conversation or discuss theological perspectives.

The Scripture says that God sent John the Baptist as a voice! It was a voice with strength and courage. He wasn't afraid to confront his sinfulness; therefore, he wasn't scared to confront King Herod's sinfulness.

Courage is the only thing we need to get the job done. If you and I have courage, we will be pleasing to the Lord as we carry out His will without obstacles! Neh'enah.

46

Perseverance! – Part 1

"Now when He had taken the scroll, the four living creatures and the twenty-four elders fell down before the Lamb, each having a harp, and golden bowls full of incense, which are the prayers of the saints. And they sang a new song, saying:
"You are worthy to take the scroll,
And to open its seals;
For You were slain,
And have redeemed us to God by Your blood
Out of every tribe and tongue and people and nation,
    And have made us kings and priests to our God;
And we shall reign on the earth." (Revelation 5:8-10)

As I have been in this wonderful season of prayer and fasting for the last 30-plus days, I have experienced incredible peace and leadership from the Holy Spirit. He desires to lead my heart in the way that I should go, and through fasting, I have found that my heart and mind are more aligned with His.

I will say more about my glorious experiences while on this fast in my meditations.

Last night as I was getting ready to give my class at our

Bible School, while in our prayer time, the Holy Spirit, in a vision, came to me and released this prophetic word over one of our students.

In visions of God, I saw the following:

As she was walking across the room praying, the Holy Spirit caused me to see a cup of water that was getting filled. It was almost at the brim and about to spill over—end of the vision.

It was here that I asked God, "What does this mean?"

The Spirit of the Lord told me, very specifically, that He was about to pour upon this sister's life what she had been praying for. That the time had come for her to see her prayer request answered. The Lord showed me that this vision had to do with perseverance.

A Bowl Full of Prayers!

In the book of Revelation 5, in verse mentioned above, the Scripture says, "...the four living creatures and the twenty-four elders fell down before the Lamb, each having a harp, and golden bowls full of incense, which are the prayers of the saints."

While meditating upon the vision I saw last night and what the Scripture reveals here, I know there is a direct connection. The cup of water being filled and "golden bowls full of incense, which are the prayers of the saints," speak of a continual action, a constant dripping of water into a cup, or a continual collecting of prayers into a bowl.

One must believe that depositing water into a cup will eventually be full till it overflows or that praying is likened to incense put into a bowl for a future outpouring. The man or woman who does this daily or continually must believe that they will get something out of it – that is why they do it!

An Outpouring!

Once an individual has a vision of something coming their way, such as a prayer request, a picture of the future, or a prophetic promise, an intensity arises deep within their hearts to press in and persevere until it comes to pass!

This must be God's divine way of praying, waiting, and persevering; until the expected thing happens!

Remember the Scripture that reads: **"Then He spoke a parable to them, that men always ought to pray and not lose heart."** (Luke 18:1)

There must be something to this specific word. The Lord Jesus said to keep praying and not to lose heart. What does not losing heart mean?

The words, lose heart, signify an emotion; it means to become disheartened. In its original Greek context, disheartened means "to act badly; to treat badly" or "to leave off." To become disheartened means to become discouraged; to lose spirit.

Here's what I got from this: When called to pray and not to lose heart, one must be led by the Spirit of God to be effective in their praying. We can only go so far praying in the flesh. We will burn out and lose spirit. To persevere means to keep at it until the answer comes. This is not easy to do, which is probably why so few see minimal results from their prayers. They give up!

Until the bowl is full of incense and the prayers of the saints, the outpouring won't be unleashed upon the earth.

Let us keep this devotion in our hearts and minds as we learn to persevere in God; strive UNTIL His mercy comes!

"As the eyes of servants look to the hand of their master, as the eyes of a maid to the hand of her mistress, so our eyes look to the LORD our God, until he has mercy upon us." (Psalm 123:2 - New Revised Standard Version) Neh'enah.

47

Perseverance! – Part 2

"See how the farmer waits for the precious fruit of the earth, waiting patiently for it until it receives the early and latter rain. You also be patient. Establish your hearts, for the coming of the Lord is at hand." (James 5:7, 8)

Perseverance speaks to us of time. To persevere means that we must continue asking for something promised. We pray until it manifests!

Now, persevering is most definitely not for the weak in heart!

People who persevere are of a different breed. You may disagree with me on this, but I have lived long enough and have known God long enough to know that unless one is willing to persevere and get what was promised, one will never see the promise in its fullness.

Allow me to share what I believe is to be the heart of God in the issue of waiting for the manifestation of any given promise or prophetic word given.

I Want it Now!

Believers have terrible habits, and it's no different from unbelievers. The practice is that they think life works like a microwave oven. People think we can turn life on and off with the flick of a switch! Have you noticed this?

I am making this more dramatic than it seems, but you know exactly what I mean. The terrible feeling of not fitting into a new shirt or pants must be one of the many awful feelings ever. Not being able to lose weight soon enough for the upcoming class reunion and being unable to fit into that suit or that lovely dress for the occasion is a terrible feeling.

There are things you can't change overnight; it will take time and discipline to see results.

The Law of Sowing and Reaping!

The law of sowing and reaping is always present and always at work! We can't do away with it; we can't erase it; we can't ignore it, and we can't deny it! We are all under its mighty hand when it comes to the law of sowing and reaping!

Yes, we will all be held accountable for it when the results come in; it will all come out in the wash!

Therefore, it would be of great wisdom to learn its principle and redirect our life by basing our newfound understanding on it. Let us understand what it means and how we can better be led by it.

Enamored with the *Now!*

For some strange reason, believers think God will give you and me what we want or need now! People come and get prayed for in our meetings in hopes that God will do fantastic work right now! That is what they say to themselves when they are driving to church: "I want God to do a miracle for me now!" Or "I hope so, and so is praying for people, so I can get in on it and receive my miracle!" Etc.

This is the typical cry in people's lives today. They need something, and they need it now!

Do I believe God can do a miracle based on people's faith? Absolutely! I believe God can heal or reach anyone at any time. People in dire need can get an answer immediately or even as they drive to the prayer meeting. I have never doubted God working in this way.

Suppose this is how you have chosen to live your life; good luck. It will soon come to pass when God has to sit you down and talk seriously regarding your life principles.

It can't be that you live so irresponsibly. By this, I mean in negligence, in rebellion, and religiously ignorant, under false teachings that move in metaphysical faith and are founded on greed and self; and then expect God to carry you through because of your foolishness! I'm telling you, it will not happen!

Walking in God's Design

When the Lord gives us a word, a prophetic promise, etc., He is waiting for us to do something with it. Let us see...

"And again, He began to teach by the sea. And a great multitude was gathered to Him, so that He got into a boat and sat in it on the sea; and the whole multitude was on the land facing the sea. Then He taught them many things by parables and said to them in His teaching: "Listen! Behold, a Sower went out to sow. And it happened, as he sowed, that some seed fell by the wayside; and the birds of the air came and devoured it. Some fell on stony ground, where it did not have much earth; and immediately it sprang up because it had no depth of earth. But when the sun was up it was scorched, and because it had no root it withered away. And some seed fell among thorns; the thorns grew up and choked it, and it yielded no crop. But other seed fell on good ground and yielded a crop that sprang up, increased, and produced: some thirtyfold, some sixty, and some a hundred." And He said to them, "He who has ears to hear, let him hear!" And He said to them, "Do you not understand this parable? How then will you understand all the parables?

The sower sows the word. And these are the ones by the wayside where the word is sown. When they hear, Satan comes immediately and takes away the word that was sown in their hearts. These likewise are the ones sown on stony ground who, when they hear the word, immediately receive it with gladness; and they have no root in themselves, and so endure only for a time. Afterward, when tribulation or persecution arises for the word's sake, immediately they stumble. Now these are the ones sown among thorns; they are the ones who hear the word, and the cares of this world, the deceitfulness of riches, and the desires for other things entering in choke the word, and it becomes unfruitful. But these are the ones sown on good ground, those who hear the word, accept it, and bear fruit: some thirtyfold, some sixty, and some a hundred." (Mark 4:1-9, 13-21)

The Sower went to sow seed, the Scripture says. This is God Himself sowing His word. Where is He sowing it? He is sowing it on the ground. The Bible teaches us that this Sower sowed seed on four different grounds: By the wayside, on stony ground, thorny ground, and finally, on good ground.

The ground is the heart of the believer. He will not clean and prepare the ground; this is the believer's responsibility. It's up to us to make good use of the earth; we must cultivate it and always prepare it for when He speaks.

Cultivating the Seed!

In cultivating the seed, one must first learn always to prepare their hearts (the ground) to receive that prophetic word or promise. By the way, you know what kind of ground you have before you!

Once the seed is in the ground, your ground; you must cultivate it by watering it. You must know that it is your promise; it is your future! You either prepare it or you don't.

After this, you wait and wait and wait, until…until you see the plant coming out of the ground. This takes time, in case you didn't realize it. Don't walk away from it; don't consider it as something worthless – remember, it's your future! As it grows daily, you are still called to work and cultivate it.

You began to be more intentional with your little plant knowing that it has a good effect on your behalf. So, you dig around it, keep the ground clean, and even build a fence around it to protect it. Why? Because it is your future!

Staying focused till the end takes work. It takes perseverance; it takes discipline!

The Fruit is Here!

Finally, one day, you begin to eat its fruit. When you inspect your fruit and see it is delicious and worthy of sharing with someone else, you will share it joyfully! Usually, if something doesn't taste good, you won't share it; if you have done your part in bringing this promise to pass, know that God has done His part! The results will be solely based on your obedience, responsibility, cultivation, perseverance, and discipline!

This is God's design for us who believe! Neh'enah.

48

Are You Willing to Be Led?

"Whether it was two days, a month, or a year that the cloud remained above the tabernacle, the children of Israel would remain encamped and not journey; but when it was taken up, they would journey. At the command of the LORD, they remained encamped, and at the base of the LORD they journeyed; they kept the charge of the LORD, at the command of the LORD by the hand of Moses." (Numbers 9:21-23)

In meditation this morning, the Spirit of the Lord opened my heart to see the value of walking with God more personally.

I have come to learn and continue to learn a more excellent method of discerning God. Let me tell you how this has become a key to my walk and a better understanding of what God expects from His servants. God desires that we understand His intention and focus on His genuine heart desire. The secret lies in detail.

Many today walk blindly with God and don't have a personal relationship with the Holy Spirit or His Word. They are not interested in knowing what God is saying; they only want to sit back and receive whatever their finite minds can capture. It is no wonder why the church of Jesus is so anemic today!

Ready or not!

As the Lord took the children out of Egyptian bondage, it was evident that God was going to teach His people His ways.

Ready or not - His laws, statutes, and everything related to divine order would be laid out before the Hebrew children. They were to walk with God through the Red Sea and into the wilderness. In their carnal mind, they perhaps thought this would be an easy thing to do, yet God, in His wisdom, had other intentions.

God's Intentions!

God's intentions are always to form Christ, His Son, in us! Never be mistaken about this. God desires to conform us to His Son and will do anything to make this happen!

I think too many people see Christianity as a religion for good people. Practice in the teachings of Christ but without Spirit! Isn't that the truth? As one man said when speaking of the lazy church in America, *We have already been educated beyond our level of obedience!*

Walking with God must be intentional. One must allow

Jesus to come into their hearts and willfully make Him Lord of all. This includes my whole life: material possessions, my emotions, my attitudes, my desires, and ambitions, and everything else I hope to be all of it - we must surrender all for this thing [true Christianity] to work!

We Must be Willing to Be Led!

In this very posture, the Lord needed Israel to be in. He needed people who would follow and not complain and whine about how rough life was or was.

For this to occur, God provided a cloud by day and a fire by night as a Guide to get them from point A to point B.

Often, we think materially, fleshly, earthly, or however, we want to describe best the life we are looking for, or perhaps the life we hope God will give us if we follow Him with all our heart. This is called following Christ for or with a particular interest! You will be disappointed if your heart is of this nature!

God provided this cloud to lead God's people through the long and weary desert. Remember: deserts are always symbolic of testing. According to Deuteronomy 8, God was testing His people throughout the wilderness, trying to find out what was in their hearts.

So, when we allow God to lead us, it is safe to say that he

intends to find out what is in our hearts. Do you see this? Have you come to the realization of this in your own life?

The Timing of the Test

When tests come into our life, we must understand a few things: One of those things is that He brings us into a place and makes us wait for a specific time. His clock, not ours, controls this particular time!

We can liken this time to a fire burning inside a furnace, and we are baking inside that furnace. No one takes the bread out of the oven until it is baked. No one works with metal and attempts to shape it, at least not until the metal is red hot. God won't do anything deep inside us until we are on the brink of breaking!

It's Not About Timing; It's About Completion!

"Whether it was two days, a month, or a year that the cloud remained above the tabernacle, the children of Israel would remain encamped and not journey; but when it was taken up, they would journey."

As I close this meditation, I have come to learn the timing of God in matters concerning my life. Whether He allows me to face a test that last one day, one week, one month, or a few years, it is all for my benefit. This will increase my capacity for spiritual authority and dominion. To God be the glory now and always! Neh'enah.

49

Learning to Advance in the Will of God! – Part 1

"And the LORD spoke to Moses, saying, "Send men to spy out the land of Canaan, which I am giving to the children of Israel; from each tribe of their fathers, you shall send a man, everyone a leader among them." (Numbers 13:1, 2)

Our walk with God is a walk of advancement. We are called to pursue God until the day He takes us home. Too often, preachers have made this walk with God a hayride. "It is easy, and God is going to make it all the better for you by simply existing," they say. To make things worse, too many believers feel they have arrived once they give their lives to Christ. We can now sit back and enjoy our newfound devotion to Christ and sit in our churches until the kingdom comes! That this is all that there is to it.

When pursuing the will of God, one must understand that it is not as easy as one thinks. Many believers have said, "If God is with me, everything will be all right!" They soon discover that as they begin to move in God's will, things get complicated, and eventually, a choice must be made if we are to pursue or stop!

Church, let me say: There is a battle, a dogfight, or as a friend of mine says, "You have to fight as if you are the third monkey that wants to get into the ark" if you are to advance in the kingdom of God and take what is yours!

The battle is real. The enemy is real. There will be black eyes, bruises, broken bones, and deep cuts, and you might get scratched. Please listen to me: A man or woman that is not disciplined in the ways of God will not take possession of what is rightfully theirs!

This can explain why many believers are still trying to get their act together in their lives, their marriages, and the other countless things that matter to them. No wonder people are weary or tired of fighting – they are not moving with God. They are not paying attention to what they want from them; they focus on what they want, not what God wants.

The Challenge to Cross into the Promise!

Initially, the people of God were unsure if God was honest with them. So, to put this to rest, God told Moses to gather 12 spies to go into the Promised Land and spy it out, and so they did.

Once the spies went to spy out the Promised Land, they came back with exciting findings.

They found out first that God was not lying to them. The land was prosperous and filled with every good thing. Listen to this: **"Now they departed and came back to Moses and Aaron and all the congregation of the children of Israel in the Wilderness of Paran, at Kadesh; they brought back word to them and all the congregation and showed them the fruit of the land. Then they told him and said: "We went to the land where you sent us. It truly flows with milk and honey, and this is its fruit."** (Numbers 13:26, 27)

When God tells us to advance, it is never to hurt us but to bring us into a higher place of blessing - always!

Remember, before you even think of what you want or need, God already knows. He will move accordingly to align us to what is best for us, not what we believe, but what He thinks is best.

Up to this point, God's people are excited about God, His promises, His blessings, and all the beautiful things God wants to do. Most believers go this far until they see how much it will cost. This has always been the deciding factor if we advance or not.

The Cost!

Listen to this: **"Nevertheless the people who dwell in the land are strong; the cities are fortified and very large;**

moreover, we saw the descendants of Anak there. The Amalekites dwell in the land of the South; the Hittites, the Jebusites, and the Amorites dwell in the mountains; and the Canaanites dwell by the sea and along the banks of the Jordan." (Numbers 13:28-29)

They saw the good stuff as they entered the land and were wowed! As they kept looking more profound, they saw the strength of the enemy; the fortified cities and the descendants of Anak, not to mention all the other tribes that surrounded the region.

You see, our walk begins with a deliberate choice to follow Jesus wherever He takes us. The cost is high and expensive – too many people don't want to pay the price, so they get what they pay for. They pay nothing; they get nothing! It makes me wonder how many people are ready to cross into their rightful place.

In the words of Jesus: **"Now great multitudes went with Him. And He turned and said to them, "If anyone comes to Me and does not hate his father and mother, wife and children, brothers, and sisters, yes, and his own life also, he cannot be My disciple. And whoever does not bear his cross and come after Me cannot be My disciple. For which of you, intending to build a tower, does not sit down first and count the cost, whether he has enough to finish it—lest, after he has laid the foundation, and is not able to finish, all who see it begin to mock him, saying,**

'This man began to build and was not able to finish."
(Luke 14:25-30)

Any advancement (whether big or small) in the will of God begins by understanding how expensive it will be to get what is rightfully yours! Neh'enah.

50

Learning to Advance in the Will of God! – Part 2

"Then Caleb quieted the people before Moses and said, "Let us go up at once and take possession, for we are well able to overcome it." (Numbers 13:31)

In our study of advancing in the will of God, we have covered the value and great importance of knowing that there is a cost to any advancement. We must realize that this is God's will for you and me.

You see, my friends; the gift of salvation is free; but the advancement into deeper realms of His will is costly and might be too expensive for some of us. You decide if you want to move forward in God by paying the cost or stay where you are present for the rest of your life here on earth.

We pick up our meditation at where the 12 spies had returned with the actual fruit in their hands and a report of great opportunity.

You would think this would be enough to convince them that they were to cross immediately, but apparently, they had a different spirit. It is here where we begin to recognize and, by God's grace, dismantle this mindset of fear and cowardness.

Caleb & Joshua: Men of Faith

Caleb and Joshua were two spies who had seen the great opportunity God afforded them. They did not doubt that the land was good; that the land was promising; and that what God had promised, He would also keep! They most definitely had a different spirit than the other ten spies.

The scripture says that Caleb **"quieted the people before Moses."** What does this mean? To quiet means to hush, to silence with solid feeling or intent. Caleb believed with all His heart what God had said and was convinced that God would give them the land if they moved forward!

Passivity and fear have controlled believers for centuries! Moving forward has never been the majority in the Christian church. Mainly, the church is composed of faithless and cowardly servants. They will not stand up for what they believe, much less act.

What Must We Do to Advance?

First, we must see God's portal or door of opportunity! Too many believers in the Christian church today are all talking if anything. They talk a big game but do nothing! We won't be able to act unless we see what God sees.

They believe they know what they should do but will not step out and take care of business. No action! This is why so many struggle in their lives, marriages, and other situations.

Secondly, we must see God's provision in His call. If God tells us to do something, He will back it up by standing by our side every step of the way. Do you know Him enough to trust Him? Do you believe He told you to act and that He will be by your side?

Thirdly, we must not see our ability! It is a tragic mistake when we look at our resources for what God can do. God does not look at our ability when He is about to act through us. He is looking for obedience. God will work through us as we show dependence upon His mercy.

Here are some traps: If we are looking for the right circumstances, the perfect timing, or for us to get better at this or that, all these are only signs of fear. Fear has been the culprit within us that has held us back countless times.

If you do an introspection, you will discover that fear has been the enemy that has kept us where we presently are and continues to hold us as slaves to its awful grip.

Lastly, advancement in the will of God will constantly be challenged! Fear has a way of masquerading itself in our lives. It comes in many ways, but let me share three ways in which I have recognized fear . . .

1. It puts us in a Comfort Zone.

    a. People like what they are doing and don't want to change; they are too comfortable.

    b. 80% of the population find reasons not to change, even though it may benefit them.

2. It messes with our mindset and releases this thing called learned helplessness.

    a. This is where people feel and say, "I can't do it!

3. Fear invites us to the Path of Least Resistance.

    a. We are always looking for the easiest way to achieve a result.

    b. Nothing worthwhile can be achieved easily.

    c. Anything worthwhile takes long periods of hard work.

    d. There will be failures along the way.

God's leadership is rarely waiting for some perfect thing to take place; He is waiting for perfect obedience to be set in the man or woman of faith.

Let us look for that portal from God to open. We will find God's favor, authority, and power in the doorway! This will be our most significant sign of moving forward in God's will. Neh'enah.

51

Beware of Lukewarmness! – Part 1

"And to the angel of the church of the Laodiceans write, 'These things says the Amen, the Faithful and True Witness, the Beginning of the creation of God: "I know your works, that you are neither cold nor hot. I could wish you were cold or hot. So then, because you are lukewarm and neither cold nor hot, I will vomit you out of My mouth." (Revelation 3:14-15)

While I slept, I believe the Lord gave me a prophetic dream. Also, during my early morning prayer, God spoke to me some exciting things regarding the subject at hand, about lukewarmness.

I believe lukewarmness is a state of the heart, a place where our devotion to anything, mainly God, is at a comfortable temperature. To be lukewarm is to be neither hot nor cold but just in the middle regarding temperature. For some odd reason, the flesh loves comfort; it loves to be pampered; it loves to oversee our emotions, and it subtly dictates our attitude, which will affect our devotion to Christ.

I know some people like to be part of a Christian ministry or church, but nothing more. They are not looking for adventures in God; they are looking for a comfortable state of being that says, "I am saved, and I am happy this way." There is much of this in our local churches.

This or That?

As I dreamt of this early morning, I saw a man named David in my dream. I called him over to me and asked him, "David, what ministry are you leading?" He said, "I don't know. I thought so and was in charge and leading that ministry." He seemed lost. I told him, "David, you are in charge!"

By the appearance of this dream, this servant of God seemed lost and confused. He didn't know if to do this one ministry; or if he was to do another type of ministry. I was able to bring clarity to him and lead him. He took charge after that—end of the dream.

This dream concerns a lukewarm heart, not knowing where to go and what to do. It can't lead with a roar because it doesn't know the sound of Lion's roar. It doesn't recognize God's leadership. If we lose sight of God's guidance, we lose everything!

Where Does Lukewarmness Begin?

"Elijah approached all the people and said, "How long will you [a]hesitate between two opinions? If the Lord is God, follow Him; but if Baal, follow him." (1 Kings

18:21a - Amplified Version)

One of the things I have learned is how this lukewarmness accommodates itself in someone's life. It doesn't come with full force; it comes very subtle and very slowly, almost like a slithering of a snake to kill its prey.

As a believer, there are things that one cannot afford to do. For example, a servant of God must realize that since he has been born of the Spirit of God, he must maintain that connection. It is vital to stay in communion with the Spirit of God. To neglect this part of your walk with God is to commit spiritual suicide.

At this moment, the spiritual life experiences lukewarmness; once it begins, it will continue to affect every part of that individual.

Two Opinions

The first thing I see in a lukewarm individual is their trend to have two opinions. They begin to doubt the very thing they once believed. Where there was once a deep trust in Jesus, doubt has now flooded their hearts; their passion to pursue is no longer that important; their desire to read the Word of God is waning; their purposeful intent to lead others to the truth in Jesus – it is now wavering between: "Should I do it; or should I not?"

Lukewarmness results from disconnection from the Spirit of God and His purpose for our life. When we connect with God, we will be consumed by His holy fire; everything we do will have fire characteristics!

Likewise, when our relationship with God is lukewarm, everything we do will be tainted by the flesh and not the Spirit of God.

Let us open our spiritual eyes for this subtle enemy to move upon our hearts. Neh'enah.

52

Beware of Lukewarmness! – Part 2

"I appeal to you therefore, brethren, and beg of you given [all] the mercies of God, to make a decisive dedication of your bodies [presenting all your members and faculties] as a living sacrifice, holy (devoted, consecrated) and well pleasing to God, which is your reasonable (rational, intelligent) service and spiritual worship. Do not be conformed to this world (this age), [fashioned after and adapted to its external, superficial customs], but be transformed (changed) by the [entire] renewal of your mind [by its new ideals and its new attitude], so that you may prove [for yourselves] what is the good and acceptable and perfect will of God, even the thing which is good and acceptable and perfect [in His sight for you]." (Romans 12:1, 2)

Continuing our truth dealing with lukewarmness, I mentioned that once lukewarmness begins to settle in our spirit, we begin to be indifferent toward the things of God. What we once considered valuable and of utmost importance no longer attracts us.

Trying to live for God with a lukewarm heart must be one of the most challenging things. To tell yourself that you are doing well when you are not must be troubling to the depth of your soul.

Here's what I said in my last meditation: To be lukewarm is to be neither hot nor cold but just in the middle regarding temperature. I believe lukewarmness is a state of the heart, a place where our devotion to anything, mainly God, is at a comfortable temperature. For some odd reason, the flesh loves comfort; it loves to be pampered; it loves to oversee our emotions, and it subtly dictates our attitude, which will affect our devotion to Christ.

No Consecration!

Lukewarmness in our life will not only cause us to have a divided heart towards God but will eventually draw us away from God. Lukewarmness will grow to be a mighty force that will drive us away from His presence and move us away from being consecrated to God. We will no longer seek to please Him in all things, much less serve Him.

Consecration to God means separating ourselves to give God everything we are and hope to be. It means we understand that life is not about us but Him! Do you understand?

A Living Sacrifice!

In Romans 12:1, 2, the Apostle Paul teaches us how important it is **"to make a decisive dedication of your bod-**

ies [presenting all your members and faculties] **as a living sacrifice, holy (devoted, consecrated) and well pleasing to God, which is your reasonable (rational, intelligent) service and spiritual worship."**

You see, attending church or special worship services is not enough when convenient. It will take more than that to walk in His ways.

The first thing one must do is to make a decisive dedication of our bodies to God, yes, as a living and holy sacrifice. Our decision to consecrate ourselves daily is a well-pleasing move to God; this says a lot about a man or woman who does this – they offer good service and spiritual worship to God. This is the first step to keeping oneself from becoming lukewarm.

Don't Conform to the Pattern of this World.

The second step is to take on the counsel of the Lord and listen to Paul. Don't conform to worldliness and its system or mold. The world is designed to kill the presence of Jesus in you! It offers nothing for the spiritual man. Don't get cornered by the enemy and start thinking of worldly ideas or vain thoughts. The devil is a liar and the father of them.

Know the Perfect Will of God for You!

Finally, as you seek God and offer yourself in worship to Him, you will discern God's good, acceptable, and perfect will for your life, family, and ministry or career.

First, you must worship and give yourself over to God's plan; secondly, you must not allow the world to influence your mind and heart; and finally, you are to walk with God so that you may know what He expects from you! Neh'enah.

For the purchase of more books
written by David Mayorga,
visit our bookstore at:

www.shabarpublications.com

www.ingramcontent.com/pod-product-compliance
Lightning Source LLC
Chambersburg PA
CBHW020243010526
44107CB00028B/1285